Wisdom
of Children

BARBARA SHEPPARD WILLIAMS
WITH HEATHER DANAE WILLIAMS

Published 2016

PCCS Books Ltd
Wyastone Business Park
Wyastone Leys
Monmouth
NP25 3SR
UK
Tel +44 (0)1600 891 509
www.pccs-books.co.uk

Wisdom of Children

A CIP catalogue record for this book is available from the British Library

ISBN 978 1 910919 20 0

Cover designed in the UK by Raven Books
Cover photo © iStock.com/Triloks
Section marker deer logo, 'Juniper', created by Lana Slaton
Typeset in the UK by Raven Books
Printed by Lightning Source

Contents

To our parents and grandparents
Edythe Lambert Sheppard
Elwood Sheppard
Ma Lambert

With love and appreciation for giving us the freedom
and support to follow our dreams.

Acknowledgements

 We would like to thank Linda Bevard for her consultation on the editing of this book and for all of her creative ideas and support, and Richard Farson, Carl Rogers, Alberto Zucconi, Virginia Satir, Ron Williams, Steve Andreas and Barry Stevens for their ideas and their many hours talking to us about the book.

We would like to thank Glen Echo Resort in the Poudre Canyon and the YMCA camp in Estes Park, Colorado for helping us find the time and solitude for writing. We would also like to thank Kent Sherwood, Ray and Phyllis Goedl, Ed McEntire, Page Donaldson, Corina Kojima, Carol Kreps, Marilyn Brown, Claudia Sitta, Jim Boyd, Jennifer Davey, Fabiana Sonnino, Pat McKee, Shanon Fernaays, Terry Humphrey and family, Joan Dyer, Kathy Krohn and all of our friends and relatives for all of their support and help in making this book possible.

We would like to thank Dave and Eddy Crocker, Pat and Bob Baker, Dan and Mary Lyons, George and Nancy Wallace , Phil and Connie Mooradian, and Bruce Hall for helping Ron and Barbara to start DeSillio School.

We would like to thank PCCS Books for giving us the means to express our ideas.

Foreword

 I met Barbara Williams in California in the 70s, at a residential workshop with Carl Rogers.

Her daughter Heather was a baby at the time, and Barbara was a shy and gentle woman working with kids, applying the ideas of Carl Rogers and Virginia Axline and mixing them with some concepts of Virginia Satir and some narratives of the Native American Navajo people. I find particularly fitting her use of 'walking in beauty', the Navajo concept of mental health and existential connectedness.

When I left California and went back to live and work in Europe to found the Institute for the Person-Centered Approach (IACP) with Carl Rogers and Charles Devonshire, I invited Barbara to offer the Kids' Workshop training to European psychologists and helping professionals. Later on Heather joined Barbara in the teaching, and they have been coming to work with us as trainers ever since, usually once or twice a year.

Initially our psychologists who attended the Kids' Workshop training were a little puzzled to see how shy Barbara and Heather were when interacting with them; their words appeared beautiful and naïve. But these doubts would soon melt away and be replaced by appreciation of the significance of their contact with the children.

I know that Carl approved of Barbara's work because he told me so when I was considering inviting her to present her work in Rome. Carl even mentioned Barbara's work in one of his books.

For many years I have prodded Barbara and Heather to write a book, warning them that their work would not be known if they did not. When the book was not forthcoming, I even sent them to Richard Farson, President of the Western Behavioral Sciences Institute and a well-known author and colleague, to give them free advice. Finally, I asked Pete Sanders if he was willing to read their draft, and I am very glad that PCCS Books saw that their work and ideas deserve to be published.

I hope that this English language edition of Barbara and Heather's book will be followed soon by translations in other languages; the Italian one, I believe, is going to be the very next.

Barbara and Heather have been doing some very good work at the IACP, with the help of Irene Hawkins, the IACP Director of the Parent Effectiveness Training (PET) and Kids' Workshop courses, and of Sabrina Maio, an IACP psychotherapist who has been working as co-trainer in the Kids' Workshop programs in Italy. Today, both at IACP and also at IACP France, there is a solid cadre of psychologists and psychotherapists who have been trained by Barbara and Heather in the Kids' Workshop approach.

What are the merits and strengths of Barbara and Heather's work? To me, it is very clear: even if the language they use is very simple, they have translated and applied in a simplified, non-therapeutic way the work of Carl Rogers, who originated client-centered therapy and the person-centered approach, the work of Virginia Axline, who developed child-centered play therapy, some of the ideas of Virginia Satir, and some beautiful Navajo concepts.

Barbara Williams has created (and later Heather helped her) what is basically a psychosocial educational intervention focused on helping kids not to lose their innate capacities for empathic understanding, acceptance, authenticity and self-esteem. Of course the hard job is to convince the parents and teachers to respect, trust, protect and promote the precious gifts with which the small people we call kids are born – to learn how to respect and not eradicate the natural wisdom they possess and the innate capacities of contact, empathy, creativity and resilience with which we all are born. Neuroscience has confirmed many of Carl Rogers' hypotheses on human nature, but still parents and schools are not trusting their children to possess any inner wisdom. This narrative of distrust turns into a sadly self-fulfilling and damaging prophecy.

Our relationship with ourselves, others and the world is an important determinant of our mental, physical and social health. People and societies that are alienated from parts of themselves relate to others and the planet in alienated and distorted ways.

I consider Barbara and Heather's work to be focused on issues of no little importance, especially today, in a world in tumultuous change, where most people are witnessing what is going on as passive observers; where people in fear are in automatic denial of the anthropogenic, destructive effects that could be soon aggravated by the approaching fourth industrial revolution, with its internet, cyberspace, smart cities, smart machines, smart cars, smart money and the commodification of everything at an accelerating pace of change.

Indeed, it makes sense to trust, protect and promote the innate capacities of our children to be fully human. By doing so we may re-learn from them the importance of connectedness in how we live our lives and of establishing healthy relationships with the life within us and around us, in the here and now.

Alberto Zucconi

President, Institute for the Person-Centered Approach (IACP)
Rome , 4 July 2016

Preface

 We are mother and daughter. Barbara has a background in psychotherapy, play therapy, teaching and social work. She was fortunate to have person-centered parents so she grew up in the mountains, with a lot of freedom and with animals, and also lived in different states in the US, and for three years in Germany. She has traveled extensively throughout the world, and has also been particularly interested in Native American Indian culture. Barbara remembers her childhood well and has always felt a close connection to children.

Heather also grew up with person-centered parents and went to a student-centered school, and she too grew up in the mountains with freedom, and was close to animals, and she also lived by the ocean in California so loves nature and sea life. Her background is psychotherapy, social work and art. She specialized in working with adolescents.

After graduation Heather became interested in working with the Kids' Workshop as a presenter and organizer, and she and Barbara worked together, presenting Kids' Workshop training programs and other workshops about ways of working with children and adolescents internationally. Heather also specializes in photography and video and uses these tools in the presentations. She, like Barbara, has traveled throughout the world and is very interested in other cultures and in Native American Indian culture in particular.

We wrote this book together. Since some of the experiences date from when Heather was very young, she has written those bits in the first person, as they are part of the story of her life. But we went over every part of it and created and wrote each part together.

It was Richard Farson who gave us the inspiration and courage to write a book that would help children carry their message to the world. Many years earlier, Barbara had read his book *Birth Rights: a bill of rights for children* (Farson, 1974), and she knew then that she wanted to work with children to help them to express their wisdom. Meeting him felt like a circle had been completed. He understood what we were trying to express and he has inspired and helped us immensely.

In our many years of working with children in different situations, we have had rich experiences that have given us new insight into their profound wisdom. Our aim in this book is to share these experiences with you so you may see the beauty and understand the wisdom of children at a deep level. We hope you will build on what we have begun to explore.

This book is not just for professionals – it is for all people who live and work in the world of children. May it enrich your life forever.

Introduction

 We believe each child is born possessing original wisdom. It is delicate and extremely important that it be protected and nourished. A child's wisdom that has been squelched can be repaired through trust and in the right environment. When a child's original wisdom is recognized, protected and nourished, their wisdom can continue to grow with them. They can also learn to see through many more illusions.

Through the ages, people have tried to describe wisdom. Today the exploration goes on. The philosopher Ronald Williams writes that:

> *For Plato, knowledge was not enough. For example, one can know how to build atomic weapons without having the wisdom to use them appropriately. In spite of our knowledge, we fall prey to various illusions, and wisdom entails overcoming illusion. So wisdom is some sort of insight that goes beyond or forms the foundation for knowledge.*
>
> *Particularly in the West, but also in Asia, there has been for more than two millennia a certain image of wisdom. Though notions of the nature of wisdom differ, the common image is that wisdom is (a) to be attained, (b) over time, (c) as the result of a difficult, perhaps lifelong path, and (d) that certain techniques or methods for acquiring it are required.*

So in this model, wisdom comes at the end – the fruit of a well-lived life. So the focus is on that end and on techniques for achieving it gradually as life progresses. The focus tends not to be on the beginning.

This is a book about beginnings. About the wisdom that children naturally possess, and about how to nurture the qualities that comprise that wisdom.

The usual thinking is that children must become adults before they gain wisdom. In this book, we bear witness to the innate wisdom, beautiful and powerful, that children already have. When you see and experience it, you will never again see children in the same way.

One of the tools that helps children recognize their own wisdom is working with them in a person-centered way.

We believe that children possess innately within them, from birth, the qualities that Carl Rogers said provide the essential 'core conditions' for positive psychological development: trust, empathy, congruence and unconditional positive regard. Children have the ability to trust, to express themselves in a clear, straight way, to be empathetic and open to differences in themselves and other cultures, and to accept other people and themselves for who they are and not for what they do or do not do. When a child can recognize and express these qualities it helps them to be insightful, to have high self-confidence, to be creative and to be resilient.

An adult in a child's life who can show these person-centered qualities can protect the child's wisdom and help them recognize and bring out their own person-centered qualities. This person could be a therapist, counselor, teacher or parent.

This book is about understanding and working with children in a person-centered way in different settings and how to help nourish and protect their natural wisdom.

At this time education, schools, child care centers, therapists, parents, medical and other systems do not always recognize or protect the wisdom of children or bring out and respect person-centered qualities. When the wisdom of children is not recognized and they cannot express person-centered qualities, their self-confidence goes down, they lose trust, they are fearful and they often either give up or rebel. The educational and medical systems are quick to diagnose them with ADHD, bipolar disorder or other labels, and quick to medicate them, when much of this medication could be avoided.

The first part of our book, on the founding of DeSillio School, is about education and covers how teachers, parents and the community can work together to support the wisdom of children and help them to learn in creative ways through using and bringing out their person-centered qualities.

Part 2, Play Therapy, is about using the person-centered approach with children from age two through adolescence. It includes case examples, experiences and quotes from children.

Part 3 links Native American Indian philosophy and our work in education and our workshops with children. The person-centered philosophy shares much with the general Native American Indian philosophy.

Part 4, The Kids' Workshop, is about the workshops and training programs we have created for children to help them to recognize and express their wisdom and their person-centered qualities, and to have high self-confidence, be resilient, keep their creativity and appreciate nature. This is a strong program that empowers children and helps to prevent future problems.

Part 5 is the conclusion, where we envision what the world would be like if politics, education and economics recognized the wisdom of children.

What if people – politicians, educationalists, economists, parents, teachers, therapists, foster care and children's centers – could all recognize the wisdom of children? How could it change the world? Children would be allowed to express their wisdom and therefore grow into wise and fully functioning adults and reach their highest potential. They could help to develop a world that would be one of different cultures expressing themselves individually and reaching their highest potential – a world rich in wisdom that would further evolve with the wisdom and potential of every generation.

Part I

Formation of DeSillio School

This chapter describes person-centered practice with children in educational settings, with a focus on the setting up of a student-centered school in Fort Collins, Colorado.

Our work has always been about taking risks; we have always worked in non-traditional ways, taking the chance that they would work. It continues to be a voyage of discovery.

We believe wisdom is different from knowledge. To us, knowledge is what we learn at school and the skills we gain through experience. We do not believe knowledge can teach wisdom. Wisdom is being aware of and knowing your own self, knowing how to learn in your own way so that what you learn is integrated with and remains a part of you. We believe most public schools[1] today fail to provide children with an environment in which they can be aware and develop their wisdom. Tomorrow's leaders greatly need wisdom, not just knowledge.

I studied psychotherapy and education, and my experience of student teaching and my visits to schools convinced me that nothing much had changed since I

---

1. Public schools in the US are state-funded and free to attend for children in the local area. In the UK public schools are elite, fee-paying, private institutions.

was a first-grader. I wanted to do something different for children – to develop a school where they could express their wisdom. Carl Rogers inspired me when he talked about his person-centered way of working with adults; I began to think of ways that I could work with children in a school setting using the person-centered approach. I also found his book *Freedom to Learn* (Rogers, 1969) very helpful.

Through many years of attending workshops with Virginia Satir, and reading her book, *The New Peoplemaking* (1988), I realized how important it is for children to be able to be congruent in a school setting in order to keep their self-esteem high and to enjoy learning.

Virginia Axline, who wrote *Dibs In Search of Self* (1964) and *Play Therapy* (1969), was a wonderful role model for me; she demonstrated the amazing things that can happen when you trust a child and the process in a school setting. I was also inspired by Barry Stevens, who wrote *Don't Push the River* (1970), in realizing how important it is for children and teachers to have the freedom to be spontaneous and learn or teach in their own ways.

My husband, Professor Ron Williams, taught philosophy at the Colorado State University (CSU). In his class he had the students read George Dennison on alternative schools, AS Neill on Summerhill, a student-centered school in England, and John Holt on US inner-city schools. Along with Ron and I, Colorado State University people from different departments – philosophy, math, history, forestry, and social work – became interested in starting a student-centered school in Fort Collins, Colorado. We posted notes on bulletin boards at the university and around the community announcing a meeting the next week. We thought maybe five people would come, if we were lucky.

But 30 came – teachers and students from the university departments of philosophy, social work, psychology and education, and students and parents from the community who were dissatisfied with the public schools' method of teaching.

I will never forget the high energy and excitement in that group as we talked about what we wanted. One important element was our desire for a school that would truly be a community school, not limited to one social class or one culture.

We had a rich source of ideas. Jiddu Krishnamurti started some of the first student-centered schools in India, England and Ojai, California. He knew and greatly influenced Maria Montessori, the famed Italian educator and innovator, when she started her first Montessori schools. He also knew Rudolf Steiner and influenced Steiner's Waldorf School. Many in our group were familiar with John Holt, Carl Rogers, AS Neill and the British infant school system. These people inspired us. We wanted parents to be involved, and we wanted children to be free to learn in their own way – each moving at his or her own pace. We opposed a graded system that put the emphasis on competition. We supported a learning environment in which children would be free to learn about what interested them at that moment – important knowledge that would become a part of them.

We met again the next week. Even more people attended, and they brought their children, and from then on the children were included in the planning. This time we focused on what we needed to start the school, and divided into groups to work on it.

- The building committee would search for a building or space where children could make noise and be free to be themselves, and which would also meet county requirements for safety and for a school.

- Another committee was formed to find out what the county requirements were for starting a private school. Its members met regularly with representatives of two other private schools, Montessori and Saint Joseph's.

- A teacher committee would begin to seek out qualified subject matter experts who also understood children at a deep level and could express that in an intensive, often stressful, environment. This was one of our greatest challenges. We interviewed the candidates intensively, asking about their background, their philosophy of education and how they related to children, and their past experience. We observed them working with children in the school for two weeks before we made our decision. Our first teachers were able to relate to the children and faithfully maintain our philosophy of education. Later we needed additional teachers and it was harder to evaluate them. Too often candidates believed intellectually in our philosophy and in our way of relating to children and could express it verbally, but they could not express it emotionally and maintain it on a day-to-day basis. As time went on, this caused problems in the school.

- A committee of parents started working on funding and grants for the school. These were mainly people from the university with the relevant experience.

- Another committee set out to let people know our philosophy and find potential students from all parts of the community. We wanted a bilingual school. Committee members met with low-income parents on welfare and those who spoke Spanish visited the Hispanic community.

There were many low-income Hispanic people living in Fort Collins at that time. Many had come from Mexico and spoke no English; some were not US citizens. They usually worked in the sugar beet fields or did other agricultural work. Often they lived in sub-standard housing on the edge of town. The predominantly Anglo townspeople discriminated against them and made little effort to understand or appreciate their culture. Younger children went to predominantly Hispanic neighborhood schools, and when they reached high school age they were sometimes overwhelmed by the cultural unfamiliarity of the Anglos. They frequently dropped out, and of those who graduated, few went on to college. With great patience, and trusting the process, George Wallace gained the trust of the Hispanic elders, describing our ideas for the school to them and urging them to send their children to us. The elders agreed.

We also met with the school board that oversaw Fort Collins public schools, and spoke to university classes. With Bruce Hall, I offered a continuing education class in alternative education through CSU. We continued these activities once the school was under way, trying to work with all parts of the community and talking to doctors, psychologists, social workers and teachers from other schools.

As I've said, children took part in the group meetings from the beginning, and when they were tired there was a place where they could play. They were very involved in the project and were eager to help. At our second meeting, the question of naming the school arose. The adults were tossing around names along the lines of 'Fort Collins Community School' when one child suddenly suggested, 'Let's name it "The Silly Old School"!' The other children excitedly agreed.

We adults liked the name too, but we wondered how it would affect the likelihood of getting funding. So the children and adults together decided to disguise the name as DeSillio School. We even invented a historical Italian philosopher named DeSillio who thought up the concept of the alternative school and was beheaded for doing so.

Tremendous energy, commitment and hard work were evident at these meetings, which started in March 1970. By 8 September of that year, DeSillio School was under way, with 36 children from the ages of five to 12, four teachers, and helpers and volunteers. The school was open to anyone interested in the educational process and in the experience of working together as a community.

More Thoughts on a Free School
(From paper by Ron Williams, written in June 1970)
It is helpful to ask what sort of person is needed to cope creatively with the complex and quickly changing world. Some suggestions: the person should be tolerant of differences, capable of imagining other situations, appreciative of the tenuousness of theories, not overly reliant on authorities, and he should possess a new sense of community which combines individual freedom with the maximum of cooperation and love. Here again I believe that

the typical public school fails to foster these characteristics. I believe that the DeSillio School will be aware of and set up to foster these characteristics.

We hope that our children will have self-awareness and self-esteem, that they will be able to take risks to think and act independently, that they will look for new solutions to old problems, using intuition as well as logic – that they will think holistically... be cooperative... listen to and understand differences while maintaining their own value system and... facilitate communication between individuals by helping [them] hear each other at a deep emotional and intellectual level.

From the archive files on the founding of DeSillio School
First, we are establishing a free, open, and rich educational environment relevant to the interests, desires, and needs of the children. We are convinced that our school should conform to the students rather than that the students should conform to the school. Students are free from forced learning and free to pursue what interests them at their own rate and in their own way so long as they do not infringe upon the work or rights of others. With a high teacher to student ratio we can facilitate personalized learning. Informal teacher-student-parent discussions rather than grades are the means of evaluation. The students' decisions and common interests rather than their ages are the basis for whatever groupings occur. The role of the teacher is to help and advise but not to impose ready-made programs and goals.

We believe that we provide a quality of education for our children which surpasses that of the current public schools. In addition to the traditionally stressed learning of facts and the mastery of certain basic skills, we provide an atmosphere of respect, freedom, and social responsibility, which enables the child to become both independent and concerned for others. Moreover, we are convinced that learning takes place best when it is individualized and is free from destructive competition and fear of failure. We now have evidence from 50 years of studies that students from student-centered schools do as well as or even better on standardized tests than students educated in traditional schools.

The participation of parents and other adults from the Fort Collins area is an important feature of the school. On a volunteer basis, parents and friends perform administrative functions, do custodial care, and develop 'interest centers' in the school. These persons also do part-time instructing in specialized areas and help with field trips. Teacher-parent incorporation in meetings and on committees removes decision-making from the hands of the few. Participation in and enthusiasm for the school is high: virtually every family is represented at the monthly teacher-parent meetings, and a recent money-raising party drew over two hundred members and friends.

We are working to make our school significantly bilingual and bicultural. We are building an educational situation in which both Spanish and English are operational languages, in which Mexican-American teachers, parents, and students play an essential role, and in which Mexican-American culture makes a valuable contribution and is seen as intrinsically valuable. Our school will provide the opportunity for each student to acquire a deep understanding of and respect for a culture different from his own. Our general desire is to have a student body which is composed of children from as many different social, political, and racial backgrounds as possible.

The school affords an unusual opportunity for research. Many faculty members and students from Colorado State University are involved in the school and are interested in research.

> *Our emphasis on new modes of quality education in an informal, open atmosphere, while unique in this area, is common to other experiments in alternative education. But we believe that we are unlike any other school in the way we have combined the characteristics and goals described above.*

The founding committee wrote that DeSillio was to be:

> *... unordinary; at its best it is extraordinary. It is not primarily an institution or a method, but a process – a searching for an optimal learning environment to help children to learn to take responsibility for their own learning. DeSillio also is an experiment in community and decentralized organization. Our children are allowed to be alive. They can express their innate curiosity with energy and also can be honest about their fears and anxieties.*

So it was in the silly old school – in the freedom, creativity, and warmth of the silly old environment, with the help of these beautiful children who expressed their wisdom and shared it with us – that our work came together and could be expressed.

The world of DeSillio

The children came from families throughout the community. Some parents were university people; some were well-educated professionals from the community; some were alternative lifestyle families. Others came from low-income families and the traditional Hispanic community; one student came from a traditional Navajo family. There were both boys and girls aged five to 12, with different school and background experiences.

I was joined by three other teachers: Terry Funk from Switzerland, who had teaching experience in migrant education and spoke seven languages; Bob Malenow, who had taught in the Peace Corps in Sri Lanka and in a ghetto public school in New York City and had a Master's degree in education; and Norm Ottaway, who had teaching experience in migrant education and a Master's degree in English. All of the teachers had Master's degrees and education certificates. Three spoke Spanish, and all were well versed in the student-centered philosophy.

Philosophy graduates Cornia Meyers and Page Donaldson were our main volunteers.

Also helping our teachers were volunteers from the university and parents from all parts of the community. People would come in with special projects for the children to work on – for example, an elder from the Hispanic community told stories about his culture and children's stories. All of the children looked forward to these sessions, and the Hispanic children especially looked forward to the days when their culture was recognized and appreciated. It helped them to feel good about who they were. A Navajo parent presented beading projects and environmental projects.

Parents willingly paid what they could afford, and they were active and involved – they held community potluck dinners, swept up after hours, and arranged fundraising events.

The public school board for our county asked our teachers to meet with them monthly to share the new and creative ideas we were using so they could try them in mainstream classrooms. They did not support us financially.

We met once a month with other private schools for support and to learn new ways of working – the Stanley

British primary school in Denver, and the Catholic school in Fort Collin, Saint Joseph's, and the Montessori school, which worked with children aged three through five. Although we had different teaching methods and philosophies, we found we had much in common as private schools trying to work outside the public system. We were supportive of each other and respected our differences.

Teachers and helpers met at least once a week to talk about each student – how he or she was doing and how we could help. We planned projects and field trips.

The teachers, always on the lookout for new, creative ways to teach, visited other schools, read books and watched films, finding great support in all of them. They also held meetings at which we helped the community to understand our philosophy.

We met once a month for potluck – teachers, students, parents, and interested others from the university and community. On these days, children would often say eagerly, 'Oh, I'm coming back tonight, and I'm going to bring my parents!' The atmosphere was warm and the tables were filled with food. The children ran and played, and then we all ate together. At the meeting afterward, the teachers described current school projects and proposed ideas. The fundraising committee and other committees made their reports. These meetings included the children.

We knew the school setting needed to be based on trust and person-centered qualities if children were to feel free to express their wisdom. So each day began with everyone, including teachers, gathered in a circle. Everyone had the opportunity to say how they felt that day or to talk about anything that might have happened at home. Those who didn't want to talk were not pushed. This process helped children with possible behavior problems to express their thoughts and feelings, to be aware of other children's feelings, and to realize that the teachers were real people, not authority figures. The process also made the teachers aware of what was on each child's mind. When a child was upset or having trouble with another child, there was always a teacher or helper nearby who could help them process their feelings.

DeSillio did not have as many rules as most other schools. Many of our 'rules' depended on children's wisdom to understand the situation. When a child came into DeSillio from a structured environment or a difficult situation, we had to wait – sometimes a year – for him or her to really trust the DeSillio environment and its teachers and students. Then the child's own wisdom and capacity to learn emerged.

It seemed to be a paradox. We saw that traditional rules often made children more rebellious and less safe, whereas in a situation in which there were fewer rules they could think for themselves – and, precisely because they did not rely on others to tell them what to do, they were generally more cautious. We realized that other people would not always be with them in dangerous situations and they would have to know how to think for themselves. Some schools focus more on control than on really teaching children, and they often have many rules or there is a constant fear that a child might get hurt.

Often when the children are in situations where there are no rules or anyone telling them what to do, they do not know how to think for themselves. Sometimes they rebel or just memorize facts or rules. We had fewer injuries in DeSillio than in other Fort Collins schools, even though our students were sometimes in potentially dangerous situations. For example, Matt and Andy were building a structure by balancing different sizes and shapes of blocks on top of each other. As the structure grew higher and higher, the boys climbed onto a high bookcase to reach it. Another teacher and I were watching and felt no need to say anything because they were being very careful. When the structure reached the ceiling, Andy and Matt sat on top of the bookcase, admiring their beautiful creation with great amazement and pleasure and a sense of accomplishment. We took pictures of this beautiful structure to put on the wall and for Andy and Matt to take home.

Heather remembers:

The teachers had a nice way of explaining what kids from a difficult situation or a very structured environment might experience when they entered DeSillio. A child might be defensive and scared and not show it, or be argumentative and try to hit or tease. By hearing from our teachers that a child might not understand or trust an environment where children could be themselves and trust each other, we were better able to understand and empathize with them and to be patient. We knew a new student would test us, the teachers, and the environment, and we trusted that, if we waited long enough, the child would come around. We often helped the new kids understand not to destroy things.

Timmy was mean on the playground, and the teachers said to just give him time. His parents could not deal with his rebellion and took him out of school just as he was beginning to change and trust the environment. The teachers were sad because he went away. The kids felt sorry for him because his parents did not understand.

I was often surprised by the children's understanding and

patience. In Timmy's case, we teachers felt we had failed to communicate properly with his parents.

We found the children showed understanding in other ways too. Field trips were especially meaningful to them. They were usually open to all ages; a few were tailored to older children, but age differences were not enforced.

Ken, one of DeSillio's first students, was young and small for his age. He was very bright and usually participated in the activities organised for the older children. But sometimes he felt left out when older kids went on field trips.

One day another teacher and I noticed that the school was unnaturally quiet. In a room that was not used much, we found the older children. They had decorated the room with streamers and made a big sign that said 'Happy Birthday Ken,' and they had brought cookies and juice. They found Ken and led him, eyes shut, into the room. When he opened his eyes they shone with brightness as everyone sang Happy Birthday to him. The older children pronounced him a 'big kid' who could go on all of their field trips. I had never seen him so happy. The children knew and expressed their own wisdom (that Ken was a person and that age did not matter). They recognized Ken's wisdom (his knowledge that he could take in the same experiences as the older children), and this event would encourage Ken to express his wisdom more. Once again, we learned from the children.

Experiences of children and teachers

We worked hard to involve the school with the local community. We arranged internships for the older children (aged eight to 12) in veterinary clinics, university settings, dog kennels and music shops. The people in these settings were very open to having these young children as apprentices.

Jeanie and Heather worked in a kennel, caring for and feeding the dogs, playing with them and exercising them, and relating to each dog and each dog's owner. They calculated the cost per dog per day. The internship helped them gain self-confidence and gave them a chance to apply math, science and animal psychology.

Heather remembers:

One day at our request, the person who owned the kennel put us in the cage, and we went through the whole daily routine that a dog goes through. It was a wonderful experience for both of us, and we really had fun.

Charlie was never interested in the multiplication tables, although we tried many ways – visual, audio, and experiential – to teach him. Charlie started at DeSillio when he was six and then transferred to a traditional junior high school (middle school) when he was 12. Ideally, we would have liked DeSillio to incorporate the junior high years, but district school regulations did not permit it. We followed Charlie closely to see how he was doing, and every night after his classes were out he would come to DeSillio to be with the other children and share his experiences with us. One night he came in and said, 'Where are those multiplication flashcards? I want to learn them, as I need them for my math class.' He came every night to study them and learned the multiplication tables in a week. He received good grades in his math class.

About junior high school, he said: 'I don't like that the teachers don't trust me – I have to get a note to go out into the hall. But I really like my biology class and all the new equipment that DeSillio couldn't afford. Even though they don't trust me, I know I'm okay, and I can enjoy the biology class.' Charlie later received a Master's degree in social work and the Academy of Certified Social Workers (ACSW) credential.

Charlie was consciously aware of his own wisdom that enabled him to learn in his own way what he needed to know. He knew what was good for him and his own growth, and he could express it clearly to himself and to others. In the new situation of the junior high school, his self-esteem remained high. He was able to trust himself, ask for the help he needed, and be open to differences and appreciate them. Charlie expressed his wisdom by coming back to DeSillio to learn the multiplication tables and by finding a way to combine DeSillio with a structured system.

One late night, a parent called to tell me his 10-year-old daughter had been crying day after day, dreading having to return to school for the fall term. Sally was a bright and creative child who got straight As in her schoolwork, but her father worried that she was losing her creativity. Her ballet teacher confirmed this, saying Sally was an excellent dancer but was overly concerned with doing everything right. She was less spontaneous than before, and her self-esteem was going down. Even though it was just a few days before our fall term started, her father wondered if she could attend DeSillio. Sally visited DeSillio for its first two days and decided she would like to try it.

After two years, Sally's father said she was a different child. Her self-esteem was high and her ballet teacher said that she was more creative than she had ever been and she was happy. Sally's natural way was to be spontaneous and creative; she had high energy. At her former school and from others she was getting messages that there was something wrong about being different and she should be quieter and calmer. Sally was struggling to find the 'right' way to do well, but she did not feel that it was okay to be herself and to be spontaneous. At DeSillio she became consciously aware of her wisdom and trusted that it was okay to be different.

Maria was also 10 when she came to DeSillio. She was a bright, creative child who lived with her grandparents in a traditional Hispanic family. Her grandparents had noticed that this formerly strong and independent child was not happy. At DeSillio she quickly relaxed, related well to the other children, and was able to express herself. Three of our teachers spoke Spanish. Members from her community came in once a week and shared stories, crafts, and games. Noting the value and respect being given to her culture, she came to be aware of her own wisdom and regained her courage, self-confidence and pride in her culture. Her self-esteem rose and, as she entered her teenage years, she felt she could do whatever she wanted.

We found that children who had previously taken behavior-modification drugs were able to learn at DeSillio without the drugs, and to mature emotionally and gain confidence and self-esteem. None of our children were on medication for psychological problems or behaviors. Each teacher was aware of each child and his or her background, learning styles, possible emotional problems and academic progress. The teachers met each week to discuss each child. If a child was hyperactive, had a short attention span, or had a behavior problem or learning difficulty, the teacher was aware of it and helped the child find resources that would help them be aware of him or herself and what he or she needed.

As my background was in the field of psychotherapy and social work, I spent time individually with children who were having problems. Neal had trouble learning, concentrating and sitting still. At his previous schools he had been defiant and hostile, and he continued this behavior at DeSillio with teachers and many of the children. He had previously been on behavior-modification drugs but was taking nothing when he came to us.

When Neal began to trust others and feel acceptance by the teachers and students, he began to talk more. One day, he said he would like to have a hamster, as he had never had one. The teachers thought this would be a great project, and I met with Neal and other interested children.

We first decided it would help to know more about hamsters. We started at the library, where we read about what hamsters ate, how much to feed them, and how to take care of them. One child asked what part of the world hamsters came from. We found a book with the answer, looked at the countries on a map, and read a geography book about the countries.

We discovered that we needed a cage. The book on hamster care gave the size specifications and noted that hamsters enjoy having a place in the cage to hide and to sleep, as well as a place to play. We found a book on how to build a hamster cage and went back to school to take measurements in a corner the children thought the hamster would like. The children took turns measuring the space for the cage and then we went to the lumberyard with our list of the materials we needed to make the cage.

The lumberyard clerk had earlier agreed to be a part of DeSillio's learning projects. The children told him what we needed – lumber for a frame and an enclosed hiding place, and wire screen for a covering – and helped the clerk measure the lumber and screen. The children watched as the clerk cut the lumber and screen into the different sizes, and then they thought about what else they would need to complete the cage, such as nails.

The teachers had never been able to get Neal involved in projects in the school before. Yet, as this adventure went on, Neal was increasingly interested and involved in every step. Children of all ages worked together as a team to build the cage and all helped to decide the measurements and read about how to put it all together and were very proud when it was finished.

Next our group went to the feed store to buy the food we had read about and bedding for a soft sleeping place. We discussed the best way to properly feed and care for our hamster and give it room to play, and the children quickly decided they would take turns caring for it. They wrote a schedule and put it on the wall near the hamster cage.

Finally the day came when we were ready for our hamster. At the pet store, the group picked out our very special hamster and decided it needed a playmate, so we bought two (knowing that someday there might be baby hamsters). The whole school was waiting for us when we returned, and it was a very exciting day for all when we started our life with Winkey and Blinkey.

This project taught us that Neal was able to get involved in the experiential learning project when he began to trust us and the other children. The children all became closer to Neal and understood him better. We were happy to be able to include reading, math, science, geography and appreciation of nature and animals in the project. After this experience, Neal became more interested in all of DeSillio's activities and took part in more of them.

Children with learning difficulties

DeSillio was set up as an experiential school, with children learning through projects. A child could work on any subject or project for as much or little time as they liked. Hyperactive children could go outside and jump on a trampoline or run around and come back to continue to work on their project after they settled down. They found a way to pace themselves.

Most children with learning difficulties feel a real sense of failure in a typical school setting. They are very aware that they are not learning skills such as reading as easily or quickly as the children around them, and they feel something is wrong with them or that they are not as smart as the other children. Their self-esteem goes down and eventually they stop trying to learn, as they believe that it is impossible for them.

But statistics have shown that most children with learning difficulties have above average intelligence and are very creative. So it is extremely important that these children keep their self-confidence and self-esteem high and realize how intelligent and creative they are. They need to know they can learn anything they want to learn and do anything they want to do; they just have a different way of learning, and they can discover the way of learning that is best for them.

Children who have not been able to keep their self-esteem high and who have given up on learning feel a real sense of failure. Their creative energy is still high. Nevertheless, they are very likely to be the children who are seen as having 'behavior problems' in school and who drop out, who are in foster homes, halfway houses, or prisons, and who are addicted to drugs and alcohol.

Some of the most important and creative people in our history have had learning difficulties. Albert Einstein, for example, had dyslexia.

Many children in our school had been diagnosed with attention deficit disorder (ADD) and had been on medication such as Prozac. Parents who brought their children to DeSillio agreed to let the children try the school without any medication; none of our students used ADD drugs. Teachers worked with each child individually and helped them to discover what they needed and what they were interested in. Each child was able to find something they were deeply interested in, so they could concentrate on that. When they needed to, the children could pace themselves by doing something else for a bit, and then return to finish their projects. This gave them great satisfaction and self-confidence: they knew they could learn and relate to others in their own way.

Along with many other therapists, I feel that very many children are diagnosed with ADD when they really do not have it. They may, though, show similar symptoms because of their situation or because people are unable to understand their need to move at their own pace.

Eleven-year-old Pete had been diagnosed with ADD and put on drugs before he was transferred to DeSillio from another school. His parents decided to stop the drugs and see how he did.

He had never been interested in math. He was very active and had trouble concentrating on any one thing for longer than a few minutes. Our efforts to interest him in various subjects were to no avail. Finally, we just watched him for a period of time to find out what he was interested in – and learned that it was dinosaurs. This opened up a variety of activities. We went to the library, where he checked out books on dinosaurs. He shared the books with some teachers and a few other children who shared his fascination, and we discovered together how many different kinds of dinosaurs there were, what kind of environments they lived in, and what they ate. On a field trip to the Denver Museum of Nature and Science, the children saw enormous reproductions of dinosaur skeletons. Back at school, we drew, painted or sculpted our favorite dinosaurs for an art exhibition, and the children wrote about the field trip in their journals. Those who could not write dictated their story to a teacher. Peter was intrigued when the teacher asked, 'I wonder how many dinosaurs would fit into our school?' He and other children started measuring the rooms and figured out how many of various sizes of dinosaurs would fit. He discovered that maybe math could be fun after all, and from then on he learned quickly.

We were able to include reading, writing, science, geography and nature in this project, so Peter learned that all learning can be fun. The teachers learned something, too; we became aware of the truth of the Navajo saying, 'We learn from our children.' What this experience taught us was that, when children are deeply interested in something, they absorb information about it and it connects at a deep level. It becomes a part of them and they do not forget it.

Peter was able to learn quickly after that experience, and he could concentrate when he was involved. He never again took drugs for his behavior.

Heather remembers:

Jeannie and I had raised two baby lambs, Brownie and Jessie. I remember the day my lamb came and the first time I held him. He was only one day old. I was so happy and excited. I loved to bottlefeed him and spend time with him. I learned how to measure the milk and how to get the right mixture of grains. Jeannie and I learned how to care for our lambs by checking out library books and by taking a field trip to a talk to a rancher who raised sheep. It was really exciting to watch them grow. They outgrew us, and it was hard to catch them when they got out. We went running after them, and sometimes they came running after us!

It was our responsibility to feed and care for them each day, and Jeannie and I collaborated on how to divide the labor. We became really good friends. When our lambs were big enough, we took them to be sheared and the people showed us how to shear them. We took the wool back to school – it was all black and greasy – and one of the teachers showed us how to wash it. It came out soft and creamy white. So I tried to think of ways to make the wool like that when it was still on my lamb; sometimes we gave them baths. We learned how to spin and dye the wool, and we made little looms, and the teacher showed us how to weave bracelets and other things. Later on, when I visited my pen pal on the Navajo reservation, a Navajo woman showed me how she wove her beautiful rugs. We also went to a parade with the Navajo students, where women from different parts of the reservation rode by with their rugs.

In taking care of a baby lamb, Jeannie and Heather learned math through measuring food, and nutrition science in connection with the lambs' diet. They kept a medical journal about the lambs' shots. They read about sheep; they wrote poems and stories about their sheep. The experience taught them to work and plan together.

Memories of DeSillio

We contacted as many past DeSillio students as we could when we were writing this book and received many replies with memories of days at DeSillio. People tend to remember the school and their experiences vividly. Many have kept in contact through the years and have reunions, even though they live in different parts of the world. After not having seen each other for years, they seem to pick up right where they left off. They have obviously shared a deep life experience.

One former student wrote:

'De silly ole school?' Of course I remember. Barely! I was five. The thing I remember most is that they let us put our chocolate milks in the freezer in the morning and then at lunch we'd tear the tops off the little milk boxes and have chocolate 'ice cream'. I tried to do it once with regular milk thinking I'd get vanilla ice cream, but it tasted horrible. So – inadvertently – I had my first cooking lesson at De Sillio!

Matthew Brittain, a licensed clinical social worker, was our first graduate from DeSillio:

DeSillio was really good in that it allowed us students to learn subjects as we were ready to learn them. Certain students were ready to go into one certain area in depth at one age and another into another subject. I recall being very interested in anatomy and physiology, and I learned the major systems of the body (muscular, skeletal, nervous etc) at a very early age. This led me to have an interest in medicine, and I learned a lot about medicines and treatment. I figure that by the time I finished I had graduate college level knowledge on these items. I then went off into geography, and learned a great deal of the world. I could name most countries in the world as well as most major geographical landmarks such as mountain ranges, oceans, lakes and such.

However, this left other areas lacking. I did not learn the times table until I went into middle school. Realizing I needed to learn this basic skill, I made flashcards and mastered the table in a few days. It would normally take a child months to learn the times tables if presented in the traditional fashion. I learned in DeSillio that I could master things easily and quickly if I put my mind to it. I was the master of my education, and I achieved my goals quickly and with little effort, enjoying it along the way.

DeSillio School taught us a great lesson: that children have an innate interest in knowledge and, when given the opportunity and encouragement to delve into their interest, will far exceed the cookie-cutter method of education as it is now practiced. I believe that, if subjects are offered to students in modules, with distinct small goals along the way, children could master a much greater level of achievement.

I recall making lessons out of common things: a trip to the dump with my family yielded a whole truckload of Lego bricks and we donated them to DeSillio. We students used them to build a small castle. I learned an interest in architecture, and that started my interest in that area, and I have now designed and built three houses, with another on its way.

We went to play pool, and I learned an interest in geometry and vector analysis. I didn't need basic math for these things, as my imagination soared and I started seeing the shape of time as malleable and flexible. Of course, I had additional motivation to see the unity of all things.

A downside of DeSillio was the fact that we had no support from the official department of education. I suppose that this is not an issue, being a private school and all.

Heather writes:

> I have always wished for every child to have the opportunity
> to attend a school like DeSillio. A place where their teachers
> truly respect them and treat them as equals. We always
> called our teachers by their first name, as they did with us. I
> knew that they were there to help me learn about anything
> that I wanted to learn. I felt supported and knew I could
> go to them for help at any time. I looked forward to going
> to school. It was a time to explore, learn and create. Every
> day was new and exciting, never knowing what new thing
> I might get to explore. The field trips were always fun and
> filled with new knowledge. The freedom to make my own
> decisions and to be myself was priceless and is such a part of
> me that I cannot imagine my life without that experience. I
> feel freedom is the greatest gift that anyone can give a child.
>
> Being in DeSillio and able to make my own decisions
> really helped me when I entered into high school. I felt
> self-confident and was used to making my own decisions
> and being aware of how I felt. So this was very empowering
> when I was in situations where my friends were doing
> things I did not want to take part in; I felt comfortable
> simply saying 'No thank you'. I did not feel the need
> to join them to be accepted by them and they always
> appreciated my honesty and accepted me for myself. This
> has also helped me in my work, traveling and being with
> different cultures. It allows me to experience and appreciate
> differences.

Phil Mooradian, who had two boys at DeSillio, said his
children loved school and assumed that they could learn
anything that they wanted to, no matter what the subject
was. He thinks his sons gained this confidence because they
knew they had 'learned how to learn'. The worst punishment

he and his wife, Connie, could devise was the threat that the children couldn't go to school the next day.

Some children had negative memories too, of times when things did not work.

Heather recalls:

I felt confused and sad when a parent took a child out of school. The parent thought the child wasn't learning fast enough. But he had only been there for three months. I felt sad that the parent did not understand the child and was not patient enough.

Children were able to express their wisdom because those important qualities – trust, empathy, acceptance, and congruence – were present in the teachers, other children, parents, and the DeSillio community. We teachers maintained awareness of these qualities in ourselves and modeled them to the children. When problems in communication arose in the school community, it was usually because one of those qualities was lacking.

Moving on

More parents became involved in DeSillio and, I believe mainly because of lack of funds, the school felt the stress and began to change. Some people believed that we needed more structure in the school to be able to receive more funding, and some found it hard to trust the process of learning and to be able to be congruent and appreciate differences. Because of the lack of congruence between the teachers at that time and the loss of trust in the children to learn in their own way, I knew that to be true to myself I had to leave. It was one of the most difficult decisions that

I have ever made and the hardest part of it was to leave the children.

DeSillio continued to change and it eventually was given another name, Rivendell. The school is strong and has positively influenced the community. Rivendell has since also generated a school named Oakwood.

Another school in Fort Collins, Colorado that succeeds at working in a student-centered way is Centennial High School, an alternative public high school. It has successfully created a supportive and creative learning environment based on self-empowerment. Students who attend Centennial tend to love the school and do very well. The school started in the late 1960s and is currently larger and stronger than it ever has been.

Most people coming out of our school systems have learned to value conformity and being alike. They have lost their creativity; they are afraid to take risks and to be different, and they fear those who are different; they try to get others to conform. The beauty of other cultures and appreciating different ways of doing things is lost to them.

Many (not all) teachers go into education hoping to facilitate children in a journey of inquiry and learning. Instead, they find themselves being trained to give standardized tests required by state legislatures.

Learning from an authority figure with a strictly controlled curriculum in such a classroom seldom leaves room for individual differences. For example, most conventional schools depend mainly on learning through seeing – but for the individual child, the most effective learning system may be seeing, hearing, or experiencing.

On April 7, 2008 Heather and I watched the last of 13 TV programs produced by Charlie Rose in a series called *The*

Imperative of Science. The panelists were Paul Nurse, then President of Rockefeller University; Harold Varmus, President of Memorial Sloan-Kettering Cancer Center; Shirley Ann Jackson, President of Rensselaer Polytechnic Institute; Bruce Alberts, Editor-in-Chief of *Science* magazine; and Lisa Randall, Professor of Theoretical Physics at Harvard University.

The panelists agreed that America is in trouble with its science education, a field it once led. Real science, they said, gets people excited, curious and creative – they develop a theory, test it, and reach a conclusion. But students and people in general have lost this perspective. Children in classrooms are likely to learn science from textbooks, memorize what past famous scientists did, and then be tested on these facts. All agreed that good science is vital to the wellbeing of Americans and that everyone, not just scientists, needs to have an appreciation for science. The solution is reform of the educational system, the panelists agreed, and this needed to start with five-year-old children and work up.

They gave this example. A class of five-year-olds went outdoors to recess, and when they returned to class they were asked what they thought the brown specks on their clothes were. Were they dirt or seeds? Chances are good that children this age would find these specks quite interesting. Each could be given a magnifying glass to look at them. The teacher could suggest planting them and watching to see which ones grew. And then they would know which ones were the seeds. Children are likely to become involved in and excited about this kind of project – although at this age they need not be introduced to terms like data, theory, hypothesis and proof – and it might engender a lasting interest in science.

This is how we taught children at DeSillio. Seeing it affirmed on Charlie Rose gave us hope that the world is ready to let children discover their wisdom.

Part 2

PLAY THERAPY

'Listen to us, just listen to us.'
(Evey, age 16)

 While I was involved with DeSillio, I was also in private practice in psychotherapy. In this chapter I will use stories from my own psychotherapeutic work to explain the benefits of person-centered play therapy with children and young people of all ages, from Cindy, age two, to Bob, age 15. Play therapy, for me, tests the therapist's creativity and flexibility to its utmost – what matters above all is being fully present with the child, and trusting the process. I believe that person-centered play therapy can help the therapist help children whose wisdom has been denied or discounted by others to trust themselves again and regain that lost connection.

My clients were mainly children. I had been greatly influenced by Virginia Axline's books *Dibs in Search of Self* (1964) and *Play Therapy* (1969), in the way that she worked with children using play therapy and giving the children the freedom to choose the activity that they would like to do and play in whatever way they wanted to. Violet Oaklander's book *Windows to Our Children* (1978) gave me ideas for original and creative play therapy tools that I could use; each chapter is filled with new and creative ideas for play therapy material.

Play therapy requires great patience, knowledge of person-centered play therapy, trust in the process, creativity and flexibility. The therapist is a facilitator, not an authority figure, and is there to help the child make sense of his or her own problems and work them out in their own way and time – in other words, to support the innate wisdom in the child.

I believe children are born wise. They have an innate sense that they are unique and can grow, learn, and experience the world in their own unique way. Each child feels at one with the world, with nature, and with other people; feels trust, acceptance and empathy, and is aware of other people's feelings and needs. Children know what they want and need and can express this.

Play therapy is one of the most preventive, powerful and exciting forms of therapy. Through it I see children make vital, basic changes in their lives as they learn to express their thoughts and feelings in a straightforward way and to make sense of things. They develop high self-esteem, which empowers lifelong growth and their ability to reach their highest potential.

Some forms of therapy are structured or interpreted in such a way that the child is unable to explore and work on problems at a deeper level. For example, frequently therapists meet their young clients in an office and talk with them as they would an adult. They may tell the child what they think he or she should do. The child is often not particularly responsive and so is labeled as resistive and unwilling to take part in therapy. In person-centered play therapy, on the other hand, children are not directed; the therapist simply observes and follows the client's lead, facilitating solutions that fit because they have emanated from the client's own process.

The traditional therapist's interpretation of a child's behavior may be totally different from what the child is feeling. Instead of trusting a child's innate wisdom, such a therapist is likely to tell them what to do. The child is likely to conclude that the therapist knows something about them that they don't know. They get the message that they cannot think for themself and, not feeling trusted, lose the energy, creativity and courage to work on their own problems. This can cause them to be frightened and insecure, and their self-esteem diminishes.

At the psychiatric hospital where I worked, the admissions staff used to joke and laugh to relieve stress. They would tell a story about how they brought in a patient who thought she was a kangaroo. That somehow got into her files. When we met with her, one of the doctors asked her why she had come to the hospital. This calm, quiet woman said, 'Well, it seems really strange, but I guess I thought I was a kangaroo.' She had read her chart a few days before when the doctor was out of the room.

This story clearly shows how dangerous and damaging it is to label a person in any way – even if it is a 'diagnosis'. Labels inhibit people from getting in touch with their own wisdom.

Tools and experiences

In play therapy, you can use anything to represent the child's family members – cars, trucks, marbles, and so on. Through them, the therapist discovers what the child is worrying about or cannot make sense of, or is alerted to possible abuse situations. Often problems that have grown from a rather simple misunderstanding can be cleared up through play therapy, and similar problems can be prevented.

Dolls are commonly used for role play. I often discover what the underlying problem is, make an assessment and carry out a treatment plan using the dolls. Age and gender seem to make no difference: some 12-year-old boys love to play with dolls, particularly in the safety of the office. It is important that the therapist is able to empathize with the child, follow his or her pace, be flexible, intuitive and creative, be fully present, and be ready to change roles at any given moment. It takes tremendous energy. Do not try to be practical – use your imagination!

Cindy, aged two and a half, was referred to me by her parents, the day care center and her pediatrician. She would not cry or laugh or show any facial expression; she sat, curled up, in a corner. She was not eating and was losing weight. There was nothing in her social history to indicate a problem. When I brought out the family dolls and the doll house, she simply stared at them. She would not talk to me. I disregarded this and started to play with the dolls myself, having them do ordinary things like eating. She watched for a long time and finally picked up a baby doll and then a mama doll and had them go around the house doing things as she talked quietly to herself. I played with my dolls and she played with hers. After a while, her baby doll suddenly and dramatically fell down a whole flight of stairs. She stared at it for a while in complete silence and then picked it up and continued playing as before.

After about four of these dramatic occurrences, my mama doll went over to the baby and said, 'Didn't that hurt?' Cindy's eyes widened but she was completely silent. My mama doll said the same thing a few more times after Cindy's baby fell, and she began to wait silently for my mama doll to come over. Finally, *my* baby doll fell down the stairs. She cried and cried, very loudly, and said, 'That hurts!' My mama doll came to the baby and said, 'I know that hurts, and it's okay to cry; it feels better to cry,' and she picked the baby doll up and held her, saying 'It's okay' as the baby continued to cry. Cindy watched in horror, her eyes big and mouth open, while this happened. And then she gasped, 'Is it okay for that baby to cry?' The mama doll said, 'Oh, yes, it is okay to cry – it feels good to cry when you are hurt or sad. It helps you feel better.' The mama doll repeated this several times to the baby doll. The baby said, 'It feels good to cry – I feel better!' and cried really loudly. Cindy said nothing but started to play again. My baby fell down the stairs about five more times and got the same messages from the mama doll, and Cindy watched with less horror.

All at once her baby fell down the stairs and cried a little cry. My mama doll went over and picked the baby up and said, 'Oh, that hurt. It feels good to cry – cry louder and louder. It feels good; it is okay to cry.'

Cindy's baby fell down the stairs about seven more times, at first crying very softly and then each time crying more loudly. This pattern continued for four more sessions. Cindy began to eat, sleep, laugh and cry, and all of her symptoms disappeared. What looked like a very serious problem, or one that could have become so in the future, was quickly cleared up. She had gotten a message that it was wrong for babies to cry, and her parents never knew where it came from.

Children work things out on a non-verbal or unconscious level. In play sessions a child may do something over and over, intensely, sometimes for weeks, which makes no sense to you. That child is working on something. If you let it play out, you will find that one day the child is no longer interested in the activity and is relatively calm. You will notice that other areas of his or her life have come together and that he or she is doing well. This often happens when a child has experienced trauma or is working on a problem that occurred before he or she could talk. The child may not remember the problem. The play situation may not resemble the actual problem situation, and the therapist and child may never know what the problem was. Nevertheless, the problem can be worked through as long as a child is coming to therapy and is present in the moment.

If the therapist can be a true facilitator in this area, magical things can happen. Susie was 14 when traumatic events occurred at home. She had strong disagreements with her parents and they disciplined her harshly. She dropped out of junior high and ran away to live on the streets with other runaways. One of their main places to live was in the city park, where they would climb trees and hide whenever anyone looked for them. When I wanted to see Susie, I went to the park and wandered around in the open, and she would appear from some tree. I would take her to a drive-in and we would talk, and then I would take her back to the park.

Susie talked in detail about how hard it was to communicate with her parents. She felt they did not understand or respect her and their treatment of her was harsh and unfair. We talked about ways they could communicate more easily, specific things she would like them to understand about her, and how she would like to be treated. During this time I was also talking with Susie's parents; I found out that they felt very close to her but were at a loss to know how to talk to her or react. We talked about things Susie would like them to understand, ways to communicate with her, and the importance of respecting her and letting her have her own ideas. We discussed how they could talk about rules with Susie and how, together, they could find ways to enforce them. At last I met with Susie and her parents and they communicated and made a plan for working things out together. Finally she was able to go back home. She got her GED and went to nursing school, and she continued to get along well with her parents.

Sandy was a junior high drop-out who had 'beat up three therapists'. Her school had said there was no hope for her and told her she could not come back. She lived alone with her mother, who brought her in for the first appointment. We established a weekly meeting time; if she could not make it, she was to call me. To my surprise Sandy always kept her appointments, and they seemed to mean a lot to her. At first I did most of the talking – about where I lived and my animals – and then Sandy began to relax and open up. She talked in detail about her friends, day-to-day happenings, and how she felt that her teachers did not value or respect her. I suggested various activities to her, including drawing whatever she wanted to draw. Her artwork was beautiful. She was also very interested in history and knew detailed facts. She became more confident and better able to communicate with her friends and family.

After six months, Sandy decided she would like to go back to school. I talked with the teachers and counselors, and they accepted her back. They also tested her and found out she was gifted so put her in special classes. Sandy enjoyed these classes and was no longer bored by school. She gained even more self-confidence. She went into high school and was the only one of her peer group to graduate. Next she studied history at the university and graduated. Once she was raving to me about how terrible psychotherapists were and how she hated them. I took a deep breath and said, 'I am a psychotherapist.' She said, 'Oh, but you are different. You respect me and value me as a person. You listen to me and my ideas, and you may give suggestions, but you let me make my own choices.'

I worked with Robert, who dressed in a black leather jacket and chains to show his love of punk rock music. Robert, an African-American, came from an area where there was much diversity to live in the small town where I worked, where there was very little diversity at that time. He felt that he stood out and was not accepted for himself by others. He also had a difficult background with his family and they had faced discrimination, which made it more difficult for them to trust others. He dropped out in sixth grade; the teachers had given up on him and would not let him back into the school. He had experienced difficulties with adult figures in his life and generally mistrusted any adult or authority figure. He was very slow to trust me and to be involved in any activities, but he did want to continue to come to therapy. After a while he began drawing and showed great talent. I suspected that he was a gifted child (and his school later tested him and confirmed it). I explained to the school that I thought that he was a gifted child and, if he were in classes where he was not bored and if the teachers and others respected him, he would be able to work up to his potential. After much work, they agreed to let him back into school. He attended classes for gifted students and did very well; in fact, he began to receive straight As. He went on to gain a PhD in psychology from the University of Chicago.

Feelings can be expressed through creative movement, dance and positive, non-competitive games. Children can make their own music (with a drum, for example), move to music, or listen to it. Teenagers receive much of their strength and inspiration through music, and it also enables them to express feelings they may be unaware of or cannot express in other ways. Many adults in these teenagers' lives only judge, so, no matter how you personally feel about the music, it helps to listen to it with an open mind. Ask the teenager what they like about a particular favorite song, or to write down the words of a song he or she likes the best. The teenager will usually be very responsive and will appreciate that you are actually listening to it, not judging it, and that you want to understand its importance. This is a rich area for therapy. Many therapists miss it, and even give advice or judge, like the other adults in the teenager's life. In general, when you work with adolescents, find out what they are interested in and go with that, no matter what it is.

I would often meet Bob, who was 15, unexpectedly on the street in the town where I live or at the mall. He and his friends were counterculture, expressing it in their clothes and music. He always wanted me to meet his friends and introduced me to each one. They were very responsive to me. Nearly always, the teenagers I work with introduce me to their friends when we meet on the street. They are often from diverse backgrounds and lifestyles. My teenage clients know I appreciate differences, and it seems they want to let their friends know it. Often I get to know their friends as well. Susie, for example, surprised me by bringing a friend to her session and asking that she be included. When this happens, I know it is important to the child, and I usually include the friend. Each time it has been a valuable experience.

Among teenagers, word soon gets around that they can trust you. As Virginia Satir said, 'I always look for the light in the tunnel or the strength in the child and, since there always is one, I work with that strength'.[2]

---

2. Virginia was speaking at a Tiyospaye workshop with Sioux Indian people, in the Black Hills, South Dakota, on 16 August 1985.

One client, Sarah, told me: 'I am 15 and I have been in 30 different foster homes. I have been in therapy with seven different psychotherapists since I was two years old. I have hated going to them. You are the first person I've been able to trust and who has respected my ideas and listened to me. You have helped me to bring out my creativity and express it and to find ways to work on my own problems.'

She was 15 when her last foster home rejected her and told her she had to leave. I had spent many hours trying to help the foster parents understand her and realize how important it was that they accept her. But they were unable to accept her individuality and creative way of being and wanted her to 'fit in', so they asked her to leave. Sarah did not want to try another foster home, so she and three other girls who had left their families decided to live together and were able to get jobs to support themselves and stay in school. I kept seeing Sarah during this time. Later she contributed artwork to a children's book that we use in the Kids' Workshop.

So often teenagers tell me that therapists, teachers, counselors and other people tell them what to do rather than trusting them and their ability to figure things out for themselves and make their own decisions. Their wisdom is denied to them and to the outside world. As a result, their trust levels and self-esteem go down. They often become hostile, resistive or antisocial and often turn to drugs or alcohol.

I once told Sally, who was 16, that I was going to make a presentation to a group of people who wanted to know how they could work better with teenagers and children. I asked her what the most important thing was that I could tell them. Sally thought for a long time and then said, 'Tell them to listen to us – just listen to us and respect our ideas.' And since then, whenever I ask an adolescent that question, I get the same answer: 'Just listen to us.'

Betty was eight when she came to me for psychotherapy. Her mother abused her during the first three years of her life. She was now living in a good environment with her father, but feelings of distrust nearly always got in the way in her relationships with other people, school and friends. Betty was very bright and had defenses against almost all of my usual play therapy tools and ideas. We had been meeting for a long time and had used nearly everything I could think of, with no positive response from her. One day she suddenly said, 'Why don't we have a TV show for other children about the Kids' Workshop? Your daughter can videotape it and I'll be the director. You don't do anything. You can watch.'

Betty was the director, set designer and actress. Every week for six weeks we had a performance for the children's TV show. Heather videotaped it and I watched. In each session, Betty greeted the TV audience and described activities from Kids' Workshop sessions she had attended and knew in detail. Then she had two puppets, one on each hand, talk to friends or adults and work out a situation using clear communication and expression of feelings. She closed by telling the children that the program would be continued next week.

Through this production, she developed trust in herself and other people. She realized she was a beautiful person who could accomplish beautiful things. This happened because she was ready to express herself and because I was able to trust her and her process without interfering. It was not easy for me. Several times I took a puppet and started to be a part of the puppet show, but she told me 'No' and continued. This showed me she was listening to all we had experienced in the sessions, even when she was eating ice cream and was hyperactive. Everything came together for her through the production of the TV show and she was able to integrate it in her own time and space. It was another message to me to trust the process.

Clara was two and a half when she first came to see me. She could talk well. She was referred by her parents and her day care center. The day care teachers said Clara just sat in a corner, often curled up in a ball, and did not relate to the other children. At my office, Clara wanted to play with the bear family and the doll house. She chose the members of her family and a baby bear to represent herself. She then chose a family for me. She chose the same baby bear for herself in each session. Clara's mother had abused her when she was a baby, and she now lived with her father. Again and again her mother bear threw the baby down and said, 'Bad baby!' Clara told my mother bear that she must have been a bad baby or her mother would have never thrown her down. My mother bear told her she was a good baby, that her mother loved her but just didn't know how to take care of her. After many repetitions of this process, her daddy bear started to tell her that she was a good baby and to repeat things my mother bear had told her. This process took much time, patience and insight, and Clara slowly came to the feeling that she was a good person and that her mother should not have thrown her down. She began to play with other children in day care and was happier and more confident at home. This is another example of trusting a child's own process of being able to work things out for herself. In many situations people might have thought that Clara was too young to do this. Many therapists do not work with young children and parents often think that a child is too young for therapy.

Things do not always work out the way I would like. Siblings Jimmy, Cindy and Jo were brought in by their parents because they seemed unhappy and were fighting among themselves. I saw them together. At first they were stiff and hesitant to talk, but after a couple of weeks they relaxed and became more responsive. Soon they began to be creative and have ideas about how they could all get along better. After four weeks, the parents came to the appointment instead of the children and said they were going to end the therapy. They felt I was giving the children too much freedom to talk for themselves; they would rather I tell them what to do. It was very disappointing for me, not just because the children's progress was ended but because I had spent a great deal of time talking to the parents about how I worked and how I trusted the children to work in their own way. The parents had even read the books by Carl Rogers and Virginia Satir that I had recommended. Intellectually, they believed in trusting the children and being a facilitator for them rather than an authority figure, but emotionally, when change actually began, they felt threatened and could not participate in the process or allow it to happen. This is not an uncommon experience.

As a psychotherapist using play therapy, you can help children whose wisdom has been unrecognized or discounted by others to trust themselves and regain that lost connection. With your support they will discover the courage to acknowledge their wisdom, use it to make sense of their own problems, and create ways of solving those problems. Knowing that you recognize their wisdom, you will not have 'resistive children' (psychotherapists use this term when they are unable to work with or get through to a child and they give up. There are even conferences on how to work with resistive children). Assuming the parents also understand and trust the process, they will gain respect for their children and will recognize their children's wisdom. If this type of therapy is repeated on a large scale, families will work out problems and violence will decrease, and children will not need to be sent to detention homes, halfway houses or jails.

Many health plans do not allow enough time for children to develop a trusting relationship with a therapist and to look at problems in depth and resolve or make sense of them. It is unrealistic to expect a serious problem that a child has had for 12 years to be resolved in six sessions. This approach is just a temporary Band-Aid. The problem comes back. A child or adolescent who conflicts with authority figures such as a parent or teacher takes a long time to truly trust another adult. Only when this trust has been established can they express their real feelings and find resources to work through their situation.

I cannot emphasize enough that the successful use of play therapy depends on the therapist's ability to integrate person-centered qualities within himself or herself and to nurture those qualities in the children. Play therapy is an art that constantly tests the therapist's creativity and flexibility. There is no one right way to do it; do what fits for you. You must be fully present with the child and trust the process.

Part 3

Native American philosophy
and our work

'Speak straight, so that your words may go as
sunshine to my heart.'
(Cochise, Chiricahua Apache Chief, 1866)

 This chapter is about how Native American Indian philosophy has always expressed person-centered values in relation to children and in education.

Navajo pen pals

Rough Rock is a student-centered school in Arizona on the Navajo Nation and is run by the Navajo people. Two Rough Rock teachers visited DeSillio and asked if any of our children would like to be pen pals with their sixth graders. Seven of our children responded, and soon they were receiving letters from their pen pals in Arizona. A few months later, the sixth grade teacher at Rough Rock invited the DeSillio pen pals to visit their class and be their guests for a week. It was a great honor; few outsiders had ever been invited to visit the school. They felt our school was like theirs, and they wanted to be more involved with us. Our teachers met with the parents to talk about this adventure; the parents were very positive and helped to plan the trip.

Another teacher, Jan, and I volunteered to go with the children, as we were particularly interested in the Navajo culture. All seven pen pals went, including Sally, Peter and Heather. We camped in campgrounds each night, and one of those nights was at Chaco Canyon. It was windy and sand was blowing everywhere. We were having trouble putting up the tents and then the rain, thunder, and lightning began. It was cold, and there was no one else in the campground. Through the dusk we saw a truck coming toward us, and we soon discovered it belonged to a forest ranger. He invited us to spend the night in his trailer, an invitation we quickly accepted. We had a wonderful night roasting hot dogs and marshmallows, and he told us stories about Chaco Canyon well into the night. I'm sure most of us dreamed about the canyon that night.

These are Heather's memories of the trip.

I went walking with my pen pal, and she caught a horned toad. She picked it up and showed it to me and said, 'Horned toads are very wise and special. They are one of our grandfathers, and we value and respect them. My grandfather is a medicine man and when I was born he put a horned toad on my chest, and that is why I can run so fast'. She could run faster than any of the boys. She was quiet and shy, and I felt very close to her. We each had alone time with our pen pal and got to know them first; then it was easier to be with the entire group. We had a huge campfire up on the mountain, and gathering around it felt magical and special. A few days later they took us to a village where we saw a parade of Navajo weavers and their beautiful rugs. I did not mind waiting two hours for the parade to start. They fixed us fry bread and I enjoyed the Navajo food.

In the high mountains, we prepared to set up camp in the middle of a large meadow surrounded by thick forest. The only other Anglo teacher said he would camp elsewhere so we could be alone with and only relate to the 24 Navajo children and seven Navajo teachers. They were very nice to us and spoke some English. After dinner we made a big circle around a six-foot bonfire that lit up the forest. People told traditional stories, drummed and sang traditional songs. At their invitation, we joined them in the Round Dance. We lay in our sleeping bags around the fire. A Rough Rock teacher stayed awake all night to keep the fire going and watch for bears. The children talked and giggled. I looked up at the bright stars as the Navajo children slept on either side of me. It was one of the most meaningful experiences of my life.

Heather remembers:

My pen pal came running up to me when we were getting in the car to leave. She had caught a baby rabbit and wanted me to have it as a gift. But the teachers explained it could not survive the hot drive home, so she and I let it loose. We continued to write to each other, and she and the other pen pals came for a week's visit at our school the next year. We stayed in touch with each other for many years.

Sally shared her experiences with her parents. Each Christmas, she gave them a book about the Navajo people and their culture, and the family kept the books on the coffee table.

We appreciated the trust the Navajo pen pals displayed in being so open to us and sharing so much of their culture. They gave the DeSillio children presents before we left, and the children continued to write. I am still close friends with the teachers we met there, and I have returned to the Navajo Nation many times.

Several months later, we invited the Rough Rock class to visit our school. Two teachers came to visit first, because the trip had to be approved by the Navajo tribal government.

They wanted to confirm that the visit would be in a safe environment for their children and a positive experience for them.

All children have wisdom, and different cultures may bring out and strengthen wisdom in different areas. The Navajo children showed their wisdom around nature, animals and spirituality. The DeSillio children became more aware of the land and its importance to the Navajo culture. The Navajo people have always lived on the same land that they are on now and are spiritually tied to it, and that is one reason their culture has remained so strong. The DeSillio parents also became more aware of the importance of the Navajo people being on their original land and realized that, if the American government ever wanted to dissolve the reservations, it would be important to get support from the United Nations and others to protect the Indian lands.

Tom Bahti and Mark Bahti, in their book *Southwestern Indian Ceremonials* (1997), describe an important cultural difference between Indians and non-Indians:

> *The most striking difference between the philosophies of the Southwestern Indian and Western man is the manner in which each views his role in the universe. The prevailing non-Indian view is still that man is superior to all other forms of life, and that the universe is his to be used as he sees fit. The value placed on every other life form is determined only by its usefulness to man, an attitude justified as 'the mastery of nature for the benefit of man'. The Indian view is that man is part of a delicately balanced universe in which all components—all life forms and natural elements—interrelate and interact, with no part being more or less important than another. Further, it is believed that only man can upset the balance.*

Rough Rock School in present times

Rough Rock School was the first Navajo-run school in the Navajo Nation. Today, several other Navajo-run schools exist that have modeled themselves on Rough Rock. However, most of the schools in the Navajo Nation are US government schools, with rules enforced by the Bureau of Indian Affairs and other government agencies. Many such schools are patterned after older US schools and disregard Navajo culture. In the past they had a terrible history of forcing non-Indian culture on the Navajo children. In these schools the children's scores on basic skills are often low. The Navajo-run schools are very different from the government schools. Often the government schools are boarding schools, and the children only go home for holidays. Bus drivers at Rough Rock drive for hours each morning and night so that children can return home.

Don Hancock, Director of Rough Rock Community School, told us the history of the school. Rough Rock was started by the Navajo Nation in 1966 near Chinle, Arizona. It was the first Native American directed and controlled school in the US. Navajo educators developed a Navajo curriculum to give children skills in and knowledge of their way of life, language and history. Parent and community involvement in the school are high. Today the school is stronger than ever and has many exciting new programs planned. For example, they are inviting teachers, students, and directors from different countries to visit for an interchange of cultures.

The schools are set up for project experiential learning and are student centered. The children work together or alone but are not competitive. The goals for the child's education are emotional, cultural and learning basic skills such as science, math and reading. These all go together in harmony and balance. Teachers determine what the child is interested in and follow their lead because, if they are interested, they will learn and remember. A community member is on hand in every classroom to tell stories about the culture and, often, to demonstrate weaving, painting or silver jewelry making. Hancock said: 'Most of our children learn by watching and observing first and then trying it themselves.' Many of the children speak Navajo when they come into the school, and English is gradually introduced.

Rough Rock has grown to include a middle school and high school. A Navajo-run community college, Diné College in Tsaile, Arizona, is not formally connected to Rough Rock, but many Rough Rock students go there and so need not leave the Navajo Nation to attend college.

At Rough Rock the teachers and staff, including a counseling department, as well as parents and community members, are involved with each child and try to find the best way for that child to learn. They are also aware of what is happening in each child's life and are ready with emotional support. When something goes wrong – trouble learning, hyperactivity, behavior problems, difficulties in concentrating – they do not punish the child or give up on him or her but try to determine what the problem is and how to help.

In 2006, according to Don Hancock, only five per cent of Rough Rock's 550 students were on any kind of prescription drug for any reason – a much lower figure than for children in US public schools in general. Rough Rock students do well on standardized tests. Many Rough Rock students have achieved distinguished awards. In Sweden in 2005, two Rough Rock students received international awards in science and drama.

At the time of our interview (this was 2006), the school was working on an exciting internet project that would make it possible for televised Rough Rock classes to be sent to schools throughout the world so that people could learn directly from the Navajo people about the Navajo history and culture. The project would be interactive so that Navajo students could also learn more about the history and culture of other countries.

In 2008, Rough Rock sent a group of students to Washington, DC for the inauguration of President Obama.

*The Mission of our schools is to focus on the Diné
fundamental beliefs of Knowledge; Planning, Harmony and
Hope. We will walk in Beauty.*
(Rough Rock website www.roughrock.k12.az.us)

At Rough Rock, the children are confident and eager to learn – a demonstration of the value of giving them a situation in which they can express themselves, identify with and take pride in their own culture, and learn in their own way.

Once, at one of Carl Rogers' seminars in California, having recently spent time at Rough Rock, I asked him, 'Do you know that the Navajo people believe in unconditional positive regard for each person?' He replied: 'Oh, yes, I know. They knew my person-centered theory long before I did.'

Kids' Workshop and Native American philosophy

My life has been greatly enriched by my own background in the Native American Indian philosophy and close Native American friends. Part of our heritage is from the Chippewa tribe, and my grandmother told me many stories about the Native American philosophy.

Because Native American Indian philosophy is so important to the Kids' Workshop, Heather and I decided we would like to speak with some Native American friends about children.

We went to the Denver March powwow, where we go each year. It's one of the largest powwows in North America and marks the beginning of the powwow season, where Native Americans from various tribes gather for ceremonies, exchange ideas, meet friends and take part in traditional music and dancing. It is a time of spiritual renewal. We hoped to connect with Justin Notah and his family; we've known them for many years. Justin and his family are traditional Navajo people and his older brother Nathan said he was happy to talk with us because he wanted to do anything he could for children. He works in Billings, Montana, with the Intertribal Agriculture Council, and is program director of American Indian Foods, International Export. He has had experience with many different tribes and many other countries and is often in a position to help others to understand Native American cultures and philosophy. Nathan described how the Navajo relate to their children:

When a child is born it is a great celebration of a new life. A child is considered sacred and a great blessing and is treated with great respect from the time that he or she is born. A child is born with intelligence (a bit of new wisdom that, if nurtured and brought out, can grow throughout their lifetime). From birth the Navajo people see the child as an individual, with their own way of being and their own way of doing things, in their own time, and that is deeply respected by the extended family, clan, community and tribe.

Throughout their life the child can ask for help at any time from any of these people and they have the support and belief and trust that they can be themself and grow and discover things in their own way and make their own decisions.

Every child can grow in their own way – no child is ever given up on. If given time, space and support they can find their own way to grow in a positive way. A child is rarely criticized as they do things in their own way and who is to say that is not the right way. We never yell at our children or hit them. We support them and suggest positive ways, through stories. Thus the child grows up in a positive and supportive environment. When a child has grown up in this environment, as an adult they never criticize other people or themself or argue with anyone else as they do not feel the need or right to. These things are highly valued and very important in our culture. Our children are not competitive as each is given the freedom and support to do things in their own way and one is not better than another. They all help and support each other and there is no reason to be competitive.

So all is in harmony with these qualities, with oneself, with other people, with other cultures, with nature and with every other living thing. The child is supported by their parents, aunts, uncles, cousins, grandparents, their clan, and the community throughout their lifetime and always have someone nearby that they can talk to or ask for help. They all know the value and have knowledge of the importance of each individual child and are very involved in their life and growth and can help them at any given moment.

The child is also supported throughout their life by the gods and the spirits, and it all comes together and is supported by the ceremonies and the child is supported and brought into harmony or a return to harmony through the ceremonies. One needs to go down to the ceremonies to fully understand. In all of our prayers and ceremonies, there is a Navajo word that gives blessing to all people of the world and all nature, rocks, and living things, and it is a word that cannot be translated into English.

We have great love and respect for our children. We would like to be a part of the experience of bringing this understanding to the world and help all children of the world.

Part 4

Kids' Workshop

A Kids' Workshop is 'a place where children are
understood and where they can be themselves'.
(Savina, age six, to her friend)

 This chapter is about a workshop that we developed for children to help them recognize and nurture their wisdom using the person-centered approach as a tool.

Nowhere is the wisdom of children expressed more clearly than in the structure of the Kids' Workshop. It helps children to support and express the person-centered qualities of trust, acceptance, the appreciation of differences in themselves and others, and the expression of thoughts and feelings in a clear, straightforward way. It also helps them to express and keep their creativity and to appreciate nature.

There are many definitions of wisdom. Patrick McKee has described wisdom as having the capacity to see through an illusion (McKee & Barber, 1999). We believe that children are born with this capacity. One example is their ability to be congruent and to give straight messages, verbal and non-verbal. Children can see through the illusion of mixed messages that they often receive from adults. Another is that they know what they think and feel and can see through the illusion of someone else trying to tell them how they feel or even how they 'should' learn. We believe that each child has an innate awareness of their own individuality, and, in a supportive environment, they can bring that into consciousness and transform it into their own reality. When that happens, they know themself, they know how they learn the best, and know how to use their knowledge.

It was at DeSillio that I introduced the idea of a workshop for children. The students thought it was a great idea and became involved in planning it. They understood the dynamics of the workshop from the beginning and were excited to be part of it. It was the children's idea to call it the Kids' Workshop. 'Adults have workshops, and we want one too. And Kids' Workshop sounds more fun and playful than Children's Workshop.' And so it became the Kids' Workshop.

The setting

The setting for the Kids' Workshop was important. It needed to be a place where the environment was secure and accepting, so that the children felt free to express themselves.

A good group size is 10 or 12 children, one facilitator and one helper, who needs to be thoroughly familiar with the workshop. We are very careful and spend time choosing our helpers. The helper can also be an older child or a teenager who has experienced the workshop in the past. Their role is to give individual attention to a disengaged child or a child who appears to feel threatened by some of the activities. Sometimes an activity brings up a problem the child may have currently or has had in the past. When that happens, the child may withdraw and be quiet, or they may become hyperactive. Hyperactivity is not unusual in the workshops. When this happens the helper can offer a child different activities that might interest them and give them support in other ways. It is important that the child feels accepted and positive about the experience. When children feel positive about the experience in general, they learn to trust the process of the Kids' Workshop and will be able to come back in the future and take part in the activities.

So that the workshop would be fun and creative, and would not rely heavily on words, I developed a manual describing activities such as art, movement, dance, music, puppets and fantasy. It presents activities in a recommended sequence that is intended to gradually develop the children's trust and enable them to express the person-centered qualities. The manual is given to people who have completed training to become Kids' Workshop facilitators.

Throughout the process of developing the Kids' Workshop and in early presentations, I was fortunate to have suggestions and support from both Carl Rogers and Virginia Satir, both in meetings and through correspondence. They were always extremely supportive, providing ideas, inspiration and the courage to go on with such a 'strange' idea. It was revolutionary to believe children are born with wisdom, let alone that they are able to express it. We often had to go on without belief or support from others.

Carl Rogers' books *On Becoming a Person* (1961) and *Person to Person* (Rogers & Stevens, 1972) helped me to understand the person-centered process at a deep level and to realize how important it is to help children bring out their person-centered qualities. I also became more aware of how important it is for a facilitator to be able to recognize and express these qualities in themselves. I remember, after attending one of Carl Rogers' workshops, being aware of how good I felt and thinking that children should have the opportunity for workshops like this. Also Carl Rogers was a great role model for me in his work with his patients and in trusting the process.

Virginia Satir's book *The New Peoplemaking* (1988) helped me to realize how important it is for children to be able to say what they think and feel in a clear, straight way, in order to have high self-esteem and self-confidence. She helped me to be aware that three-year-old children can do this and how important it is for them to keep this ability as they grow. She said: 'High self-esteem is the greatest gift you can give to a child.'[3] Through her seminars and workshops, she was a role model in her complete congruence when relating to people and in the way she treated children as totally equal with adults.

When I was teaching in DeSillio School I had the opportunity to observe the children at different ages and noticed how often the children were able to express themselves easily and had high self-confidence when they were younger, and how this ability seemed to lessen as they became older. For me it was an ideal setting to start putting together the Kids' Workshop.

During that time, Carl Rogers wrote about the Kids' Workshop in *A Way of Being* (1980). It was one of six vignettes he described as 'snapshots of experiences from which I have learned deeply'. I felt very honored to be included.

The first meetings

When I was ready to begin, I offered the workshop to seven DeSillio children, ranging in age from five to 12. I introduced it this way: 'This is a Kids' Workshop where we will do activities and have fun. I believe children know and can say things that adults do not know or have forgotten how to

3. Virginia was speaking at a Tiyospaye workshop with Native American Indian people in the Black Hills, South Dakota on 12 September 1980.

say. Some adults have even forgotten how to play. You are very wise, and you know how you feel. You can say what you think and feel in a clear way. You'll be able to keep these abilities as you grow; you will always have them. So this is a place where we can be free to be ourselves.'

I will never forget the expressions on their faces. They watched me intently, with big eyes, and a couple of them nodded in agreement. I knew they recognized wisdom within themselves. They knew exactly what I meant and I did not need to explain any more. These children were very involved throughout the workshop.

A colleague and friend, Kent Sherwood, and I decided that we would work together to present the Kids' Workshop to the community. Kent had helpful experience in community organizing. We gave a presentation to eight children age five to 12 who came from the general community. At the end of the first day a 10-year-old boy said, 'I never understood straight and mixed messages before. Now I understand myself and other people better.'

We were excited and ready to offer the workshop to the community. With Kent acting as a consultant, I talked to many people in the community about the Kids' Workshop. I went to different schools and talked to principals, teachers and counselors. I talked to community centers, churches and colleagues. Surprisingly, I found little acceptance of what I thought was an incredible idea.

I often strongly pointed out that the Kids' Workshop was a prevention program and helped to build resilience. When children can say what they think and feel in a clear, straight way, their self-esteem is high and they have energy to make sense of difficult situations they might be in. They can use their creative energy to work things out on their own, and if they have trouble they have the confidence to ask for help. And high self-esteem helps them resist involvement with drugs and alcohol. Sometimes people could understand the prevention component of the Kids' Workshop, but I was often asked if I would work with children who already had problems with drugs and alcohol. I said, 'Yes, but I would rather work with them before they have the problem.' The money was available to work with children who already had problems, but no money was available for prevention.

Some felt these ideas were just too simple or that they were impossible and would not work. Others were defensive, even hostile, about the idea that children have wisdom.

It was often difficult to find the energy to keep believing what we knew was true, and to trust the process. In a down moment, I received a letter from Carl Rogers asking for permission to publish a letter I had written to him a few months earlier. He wanted it for his book, *A Way of Being*. This was a great source of renewal for me. (As mentioned above, the Kids' Workshop is one of the six vignettes in this book.) I often thought of his reaction to my letter:

> *To me this is a revealing account of the struggle that*
> *any truly innovative idea goes through. At first there is*
> *denial and it is seen as ridiculous and impossible. When*
> *evidence is offered that it is possible, it is still not accepted*
> *by the community at large. We all profess a great interest*
> *in the welfare of children and in the improvement of*
> *children's adjustment. Yet a program that promotes both*
> *is completely unacceptable to most people, because it*
> *threatens conventional ways of thinking, conventional*
> *power relationships, and conventional institutions. I see a*
> *long tough road ahead for this very promising project.*
> (Personal communication)

Carl Rogers later wrote this reference for the Kids' Workshop:

*I have had extensive contact with Barbara Williams,
intensively in workshops and also through considerable
correspondence, and I have followed her work carefully.
I believe that the workshops conducted by her for young
children are a truly innovative idea, and are very helpful
in promoting development and personal growth. Young
children are especially open to such experiences and profit
very much from them. Very positive changes have resulted
from this workshop. I see it as something which could be
used as a significant preventive measure.*

We continued presenting workshops, doing all our own
promotion. It was hard work, but worth it when we saw how
much they meant to the children who attended.

Heather first experienced the Kids' Workshop as a child.
Later she became a helper and then a co-presenter. We
offered the workshop many more times to the community
and also presented workshops in the Navajo Nation.

Not all of our experiences were positive. Once a
colleague and I had what we thought was a brilliant idea
– to videotape a Kids' Workshop, and I would be filmed
explaining the process and philosophy both before and after
the workshop. This would provide us with a professional film
to show people to let them know what the Kids' Workshop
was and the process involved. Ten children between eight
and 12 and their parents agreed to appear in the film. We
had everything prepared. We had three helpers with whom
we had met and carefully explained the philosophy of the
workshop. We hoped everything would be perfect, but we all
kept in mind the importance that the experience should be
positive for each child. The staff members kept that thought

highest in their minds throughout, and they did a fantastic job. But we soon realized this was not going to be easy. Three hyper boys felt threatened by the situation and maybe even by the activities and the photographer. One of the first activities suggests that the children shut their eyes and think of their favorite animal and imagine what they like best about it. I think these boys did not trust the situation enough to shut their eyes or to let themselves imagine. The activity also asked them to draw their animal, and I think they did not feel they could draw well enough. When they felt threatened, the hyperactivity increased and they encouraged one another.

I had been presenting workshops for a long time by then, so I had many resources. I tried them all. Nothing worked. One helper took the children who did not want to do the exercises outside to play ball. Another helper asked the children what else they would like to do, suggesting art and even Game Boy, but that didn't work. All but three of the children became more and more hyper.

So we all had cookies and juice, and I read *The Original Warm Fuzzy Tale* by Claude Steiner,[4] with a puppet, and we all went home. All of the children managed to leave feeling positive about the experience. The staff were totally exhausted and couldn't help but be disappointed that they could not accomplish more with the children. The videographer didn't understand at all and was totally dismayed.

All the children came back later and were able to concentrate and take part in the workshop. I heard Carl Rogers' voice in my head: 'Trust the process.'

---

4. *The Original Warm Fuzzy Tale* tells how everyone has an endless supply of warm fuzzies that can be used to express warm feelings. The story helps children identify the deep feeling we all have of wanting to be liked and loved and helps them understand that these feelings are much the same all over the world.

Taking risks, failure and flexibility

The workshops do not always work out as you would like, and you may not know why. What matters is to stay with the thought that it's ok to make mistakes. Even if nothing else works out, the children will still enjoy the cookies and juice!

Every workshop involves risk. You will have no way of knowing how the children will react. They may have problems that cause them to feel threatened by a workshop activity. Whatever happens, the important thing is to try to make it a positive experience for the child. In our training programs, we emphasize to new facilitators the importance of recognizing that they are taking a risk, and we encourage them not to be afraid to do so. Often they can learn from their failures.

Our whole work has involved risk, working in non-traditional ways and taking chances, hoping things will work. It has been and continues to be a voyage of discovery, one we hope that readers of this book will also take.

We designed the Kids' Workshop to be flexible so it can fit into many different situations and time slots. For example, it can be presented at school as part of a class for an hour or an hour and a half. Or it can be presented for three hours in a community center on a Saturday. Most often we present the shorter session once a week for six or eight weeks. Children want to repeat the Kids' Workshop again and again; they seem never to tire of the same activities.

Lucia, who was 11, came to the demonstration group that we offered twice a year in Rome. She had been coming to the demonstration group since she was six years old, so had repeated the exercises many times. Each time she seemed more involved. Each time she drew a cat as her favorite animal. Each year the cat was a bit different. I saw her in a restaurant later that night, and she said she would like to come to the next session. I asked if she ever became tired of the same activities. She said, 'Oh, no, they are always different for me, and I always learn something different from my cat'.

In Colorado, I met a former workshop attendee, Bill, when I was walking past a bike shop where he was working on his bike. Now 16, he had been to many Kids' Workshops between the ages of eight and 12. He asked when I was giving another workshop and said he would like to come again. I invited him to come to my next session as a helper, and he served in that role for several workshops during the next two years. He knew the workshops so well that he did an excellent job, and he enjoyed re-experiencing the activities. And the younger children really liked him.

The ideal is to present the Kids' Workshop in a school or other everyday, natural setting where children can repeat it twice a year from the time they are three years old until they are 12 or older. This is being done in Italy and is working very well; facilitators there are enthused about it. Children who make the Kids' Workshop a regular part of their life are very strong and confident by the time they become teenagers.

Kids' Workshop abroad

In 1979, Carl Rogers and two of his closest collaborators Charles Devonshire and Alberto Zucconi founded the Istituto dell'Approccio Centrato Sulla Persona (IACP) – in English, the Institute for the Person-Centered Approach – in Italy. Alberto Zucconi is the director of this very successful institution, one of the largest person-centered training institutes in the world. Carl Rogers once told me he thought the world would learn about his work through Alberto and the IACP.

Alberto first heard about the Kids' Workshop in a seminar with Carl Rogers at Mills College in Oakland. Throughout all the ups and downs with the workshops, Alberto has believed deeply in its importance for children worldwide.

We first visited Rome at Alberto's request to present our seminars to people taking IACP's training programs. IACP has two intensive training programs that teach the person-centered philosophy: a four-year program and a two-year program. We initially coordinated our work in Italy with Vincenzo Grazziani, who was the coordinator of the Kids' Workshop training program.

Our first presentation was in Trento, in the Alps. It was a general three-day seminar, during which we described to 25 attendees how we work with children in different settings. We were nervous about not speaking Italian, and our interpreter Claudia Sitta was a tremendous help. We were concerned about whether our ideas would translate across cultures. We thought they would, but this was our first try.

The night before the seminar began, I was out walking, looking at the Alps and trying to center myself, when an Italian psychiatrist came up to me and said in English, 'I'm glad you are here. I have read your letter in Carl Rogers' book *A Way of Being*, and I have come all the way from Sicily to see if what you say about children is true and to see if it really works.'

I needn't have worried (it was a good lesson in trusting my own wisdom and being willing to take risks): people were responsive to the seminar and it was very successful. Back in Rome, Alberto invited us to return to Italy and give more presentations. This made both Heather and me very happy. Italy is such a beautiful country, with such warm and accepting people.

After Trento, we gave a similar presentation at IACP in Rome. In the US, we continued to present Kids' Workshop for children, and our general workshops, Ways of Working with Children, teaching adults how to work with children in different settings.

Heather and I returned to Italy once or twice a year for these presentations in Rome, in the north of Italy, and in Sicily in the south. A few years later Carol Kreps joined our Kids' Workshop staff to help us in Italy with photography, art and graphic design for our materials.

Later we presented papers at conferences and gave presentations in community centers and schools throughout Italy for both parents and teachers. Either Claudia Sitta or Francesca Graziani was our interpreter and traveled with us. We learned how important the interpreter is: besides translating, she conveys the core meaning of the program and influences how the people perceive it.

In the early days, I was asked to give a two-hour evening presentation at the University of Perugia that I expected would be for students. One way I try to remain calm before presentations is by not thinking about them on the day I present. On that day, a university representative met us and drove us around the walls of the town and up the mountain to the beautiful university. On the way he remarked, 'I hope you are good. We've advertised your talk on TV and radio, and we have high expectations. It is open to everyone, and there will be many people from everywhere.' I closed my eyes and tried to think of the mountains of Colorado, the children, my friends, the Navajo... any and all who give me strength and courage.

I first met the heads of department at the university and then walked into a huge auditorium filled with a standing-room-only audience: school and government officials, the city mayor, professors, teachers, parents, students, and children. People wore earphones, and the presentation was translated into five languages. There were television cameras! I was unprepared for this, and it was hard not to let fear overcome me. I sat on a platform above the audience with Vincenzo, Francesca and three university officials. It was all very formal. Before I spoke, a university official approached me on the platform and asked me to demonstrate a typical Kids' Workshop session. I felt I was in an unreal setting. This was not a small, secure environment with children. How could I do it? I began, and the audience listened quietly.

About three-fourths of the way into it, Vincenzo said to me, in a soft voice, 'Use the puppets!' (I often use puppets to communicate with children.) So I fit the puppets into my demonstration, explaining how and why I use them, and then gave a short demonstration of how they could express feelings and convey straight messages. Through the puppets I began to relax.

I then told the audience about the Kids' Workshop and asked if any children would like to help me demonstrate it. About a dozen children of all ages, five years old to adolescence, joined me in a circle on the floor. Francesca was my interpreter. I thanked the children for helping me. I told them that many of the people here tonight had forgotten what it was like to be a child and how to play, and they were trying to remember. I presented some of the Kids' Workshop activities, which involved drawing, moving and dancing, and we worked with the puppets. Then I told Claude Steiner's

The Original Warm Fuzzy Tale and the children made warm fuzzies out of different materials.

The children were very involved. At the closing of the demonstration, one child asked if she could take the puppets to some of the people in the audience and show them how to play with them. I said yes, and all of the children picked up puppets and, unafraid, took them to people in the audience – parents, other students, teachers and officials alike. The head of the university was playing with puppets and the children and enjoying it. All formality disappeared and everyone could be himself or herself. People were very moved. They saw the wisdom of children that night. At the end there was standing applause. After the two-hour presentation, the head officials, no longer formal, took us through the beautiful narrow lighted streets of the ancient walled city. We had dinner and they bought us candy.

Another time I was asked to give a presentation for parents in a small school in the mountains near Rome. The school was both a pre-school and elementary school for children ages three through 12. About 25 adults, mostly parents, attended, as well as some of the students. Because people from various countries worked in the area, the school wanted to be sensitive to different cultures. I focused my presentation on activities that encourage an appreciation for being different and that give children high self-esteem and help them feel good about their culture. I gave a puppet demonstration and conducted other workshop activities for the children. Adults and children were very responsive, and a five-year-old girl and boy from Saudi Arabia presented me with a beautiful bouquet of two dozen roses.

After the presentation, some of the parents told me their children had really liked the presentation and had told them it made them feel good about themselves. The parents worked for a Saudi Arabian television station in town, and they wanted to present a Kids' Workshop series that could be televised to Arab countries. They thought people there would be very responsive to the Kids' Workshop and the program. I had to go back to the US two days later, so I was disappointed not to be able to follow through with this project. This experience meant a great deal to me. It reaffirmed my belief that all cultures are ready to see and experience the wisdom of children.

France was the second country to develop a strong Kids' Workshop program, through the Person-Centered Institute of France, directed by Olga and Patrick Kaufmann and founded by Charles Devonshire and Alberto Zucconi.

Kids' Workshop facilitator training programs

The Kids' Workshop facilitator training programs have spread from Italy to France and the US and many other countries are interested in starting them. The programs are tailored to the needs and culture of each country.

The training is presented through theory, experimental exercises, hands-on experience and a demonstration of a Kids' Workshop. We present certified training programs to train people to become facilitators for the Kids' Workshop. Each participant receives a manual for the program. There are two separate sessions; after the first session the participants can present their own Kids' Workshop, and when they return for the second session they can share their experiences with the group. On completion trainees receive an international certificate to be a facilitator for the Kids' Workshop.

The facilitator training program helps participants to make their own search for and expression of inner wisdom, recognize that wisdom in children, and encourage the children to express it. In addition, participants can help the outside world to recognize and accept the wisdom of children.

As the facilitators observe the children's wisdom, they are often reminded of the wisdom they had when they were children. One man in the training program, who worked with computers and had always been intellectual and serious, learned to play, and he played with puppets throughout the rest of the workshop. His friends in the group said they had never seen him so happy and lighthearted. He vowed to play more with his son and nephews; he obviously continued to enjoy it because, when we saw him a couple of years later, he was still playing!

Often, participants who experience the wisdom of children during the training program find it a dramatic and emotional experience. During the first session of our program, Susan told us she had always been quite strict with her three children. She felt that none of them were very happy, and her 12-year-old son was developing problems at school that he hesitated to talk about. At the end of the first session, she tearfully asked the group if it was too late for her to change course with her own children. The group assured her that it was not, and suggested how to be with her children.

At the second part of the training program four months later, Susan reported increased respect, acceptance and empathy among her family members. She had told her children that she wanted to be less strict, to listen to them more, and to understand them as individuals. It would not be easy for all of them, but would they like to try? All three children said yes. With patience, meetings, and use of puppets to express ideas, they were able to change as a family. The children could talk to her more easily, and the boy solved his problems at school.

The activities are fun and the facilitators learn by exploring their own wisdom and getting in touch with the child part of themselves. They go through the manual that we give them at the start, which tells them what the Kids' Workshop is and how to present it in different settings. It also has all the Kids' Workshop activities in it and explains the purpose of each one. The participants experience the activities of the children as children themselves, so the process can become a part of them. The activities in the manual are presented to the participants in the same way that a facilitator would present them to a group of children in the Kids' Workshop, so the participants will know and feel what the children may experience. An example is the activity of introduction, where the facilitator gets the children to stand around him or her in a circle, and each child whispers their name and favorite kind of food to the child next to them, and then the second child shares this information with the group. The participants quickly discover how much easier it is to talk about someone else rather than yourself, particularly when you are very shy, as children often are.

As a part of the first part of the training session, we present a demonstration workshop with seven children for the participants to observe. That way they can watch the children participating in the same activities that they have tried themselves. This is a valuable and insightful experience for the participants.

After the attendees are certified to facilitate Kids' Workshops, they return for continuing education seminars and to share support, inspiration and new material. Irene Hawkins has developed very creative materials for the

Italy programs and these materials are being used in other countries.[5,6]

As a facilitator in the Kids' Workshop, you can change a child's life. You can help a child to know themself, know what they want, and know what they think and feel. They will be able to express themself in a clear way and will believe in themself; their confidence and self-esteem will be high. They will be able to make sense of and solve many of their own problems – and if they can't, they will be able to ask for help.

When a child can express their wisdom they feel great freedom, confidence, creativity and joy. When adult and child together can recognize and support the child's wisdom, there is great power and beauty.

Kids' Workshop in different settings and cultures

I was in the Kids' Workshop when I was nine, and now I am 21. It was obviously very important to me, because it is the most vivid of my childhood memories. I remember the activities in detail and the feeling of how much they helped me and how good I felt.
(Lana B)

---

5. You can find out more about the Italian Kids' Workshop at www. kidsworkshop.it The website also describes the workshop and provides a list of certified facilitators so you can find a facilitator in your area, and there are some excellent video clips. There is also a CD-ROM that describes the Kids' Workshop, which is given to schools, community centers, parents, and other interested people. Some of the resources developed for the Italian Kids' Workshop can also be downloaded at http://bit.ly/2ctpeqq (accessed 31 August 2016).

6. Our website is www.kids-workshop.com. There is also a Facebook fan page for Kids' Workshop International, with a section where facilitators can exchange ideas (see bibliography).

Diana had been working with street children who lived in one of the most dangerous and high-crime parts of her town, in Italy. She was a teacher and counselor in a middle school for high-risk children. To begin with, the trust level of these children was very low and positive experiences were rare, but that began to change when they attended a Kids' Workshop. The children responded to and appreciated the activities; some of the teenage boys worked out their communication problems by using puppets. Once the children began to trust and express their feelings and wishes, they got along much better with each other and felt better about themselves. At the end they were eager to be involved in another workshop. Seeing this, Diana's colleagues, who had doubted the workshop's effectiveness, asked her questions and were open to ideas.

Diana was the only teacher in the school who had nothing stolen from her, and she often found her car freshly washed when she left for the day (unlike some other teachers, who even had their cars stolen). Diana was able to trust the wisdom of these children, who had many different problems, lifestyles and cultures. The children recognized her belief in them, which enabled them to let their own wisdom come out.

Diana made a presentation about her work at a seminar in Rome where people who had been trained as Kids' Workshop facilitators returned for their continuing education. Listening to her, other facilitators saw new possibilities and felt new inspiration, and their ideas helped Diana to feel good about continuing her work. These seminars are strong support groups, the effects of which last long after the meeting ends.

We presented a Kids' Workshop at a refugee camp in France for a French training group. Each child came from a different country and each spoke a different language, but everyone spoke some French. The boys and girls were aged four to 12, and they came from Russia, Iran, India, Africa and Sri Lanka. This was the first time that we had presented the Kids' Workshop with children who had so many differences and also with children who had already been through trauma and problems in their lives. It was hard to get permission from their teacher, who believed the children were too hyperactive, and to explain the Kids' Workshop to her. She finally agreed that the children could attend if she could come and watch.

We were nervous. Some in the group thought we should not try it, that it would be disastrous because the children had experienced such traumatic situations and their trust level was extremely low. We realized the risk but decided to go ahead with the presentation. I left the room to meet the children before they came in. I told them my name was Barbara. I said I was very happy they had come to the workshop and thanked them for coming. I told them that there were some people in the other room who really liked children and wanted to make all children happier. Many of these adults, I added, had even forgotten how to play, and I suggested that the children could teach them.

We came into the room and sat in a circle on the floor. Fifteen adults sat behind us in chairs. I told the children a little more about the Kids' Workshop, and I introduced them to Heather and asked if it would be all right if she videotaped them. They all silently agreed. They quickly became very involved in the activities. They were calm and thoughtful, concentrating deeply, and they quickly understood the concepts of the workshop. They were not bothered by the watching adults or the unfamiliar languages that I and the translator spoke. They nearly always looked at me, rather than the translator, who was speaking their own language. I believe this is because of the power of non-verbal communication.

The presentation lasted 90 minutes, which was longer than we had expected. The children looked very happy when they left, and for us and for those who had observed it, it was an incredible and very moving experience. The teacher later told us she had chosen her most hyperactive children, without our knowledge, 'to see what you would do with them'. The school staff believed the children were hyperactive and could not concentrate. Their calm concentration and involvement were new to the teacher; she had not believed it possible. She said they were calm the rest of the day. They talked about the Kids' Workshop and kept their warm fuzzies and the pictures they had drawn. Even though these children came from very different cultures and spoke different languages, they could communicate during the exercises because they were experiencing things that came from their emotions and inside themselves. They found they could have fun and relate to each other in a positive way. They felt secure and good about themselves and felt good about each being different in some ways.

In Rome we worked with children in a neighborhood of recently relocated refugee families from China, India, Bangladesh, Egypt, Peru and Iraq. Once again these children responded to the Kids' Workshop in a positive way and we received much the same responses as we had from other groups.

In Italy, the US, France, Spain, Switzerland and Belgium, people are presenting the Kids' Workshop in a multitude of settings: schools, offices, community centers, churches, corporations, hospitals, day care centers, other children's groups, sports, theater and film groups. Other workshops are conducted with at-risk children in the streets of Naples, Venice, and other cities. People are also presenting them in Gypsy and refugee camps and through Doctors without Borders. A successful school in Messina in Sicily was developed according to the Kids' Workshop philosophy. The workshops are being presented to teenagers and adults as well as to children. The adult workshops are much like the children's workshop, and adult participants do the same art and puppet activities.

I like to get feedback quotes from children in different settings, because it shows me how the children are responding to the workshop. It is important to have the children's direct words, which can be very powerful. A common thread links the quotes we receive from children, no matter the setting, country or culture. For example, they all appreciate learning the distinction between straight messages and mixed messages. A mixed message is when words say one thing, the tone of voice says something else, and the body language expresses something different, giving you as many as three conflicting messages. When this happens you do not know whether to believe your eyes, ears or feelings and you feel confused and usually bad about yourself. A straight message is when the words you speak express the same thing as your tone of voice and body language. When you receive a straight message you hear the same thing as you see and feel. So the message is clear and you feel that you have understood and you feel good about yourself.

Children who participate in the Kids' Workshops come from very diverse cultures. There are Gypsies in almost every country. In European countries, Gypsies are among the most discriminated against groups of people. They are often poor and have very little education. The children tend not to trust people outside their culture. Gypsies are nomadic and often live in camps; their roots are not in a specific country but in the strong Gypsy culture. They have their own religion and language. Different groups have different dialects. We have always been fascinated by and have greatly appreciated the depth of the culture, the strength and passion of the people, and their deep belief in individuality and freedom.

Italian children from public and private schools attend the Kids' Workshop. Some of the schools are very structured, and others are more open. Some children are from wealthy families and some are from middle and lower-income families. Most have close family ties, although some experience problems associated with divorce and other issues. Most are Catholic. They have a strong Italian culture and tend to be very expressive and express their emotions easily and say what they think and feel.

In Italy, many facilitators are presenting Kids' Workshops with street children from low-income families where violence is a problem. These children also have a low trust level. They speak different dialects of Italian.

The French children who attend workshops are from both private and public schools and from wealthy and middle- and low-income families. The schools are usually quite structured. French culture is strong and families are usually close, with the usual family problems. French children tend to be calm, shy and polite. When they express their feelings they tend to be very articulate and can express them in a profound way. Most of the French children are Catholic. Workshops are also presented for high-risk and 'problem' children in France. Psychologists, doctors and social workers incorporate the workshop into their practices, as does the Doctors without Borders organization.

How is it that, no matter their family situation or culture, children have the same positive reaction to the Kids' Workshop? I believe it is because the children are in a setting and an environment where they feel comfortable and safe. They are with a facilitator who has integrated the person-centered qualities within herself and who respects children and can help them to discover and express their wisdom. Children recognize that the activities of the Kids' Workshop reach out to parts of themselves. The activities feel natural and the children enjoy them, and the activities can help the children to express their wisdom to themselves and to others.

It is important that children are able to express themselves in terms of their own culture – to feel confident and good about being different. They need to be assured that they can express their wisdom in their own way and in their own time and through the richness of their own culture. In the workshops the children often discover a universal wisdom they can express – for example, that feelings are the same inside, even though people are different on the outside.

In her book *The New Peoplemaking,* Virginia Satir (1988) says: 'We recognize each other in our sameness and grow in our differences.' Inside we are all the same. We all have feelings; we want to grow and learn, to be loved and liked, to have friends, to have fun, to be happy. On the outside we are all different. We are different colors, we speak different languages, and we do and believe different things. The differences can be exciting, interesting and fun.

Children's eyes are clear. They experience another person as simply another person, not thinking of race, culture, or religion. Heather remembers this childhood feeling: 'I remember seeing snow, bright and vivid, and being excited about it and its uniqueness – not thinking it was good or bad, just appreciating it as it was. I saw people in the same way.' Through support and a positive environment, Heather was able to keep this ability as she grew into adulthood. A corollary to this phenomenon is that children can appreciate differences without fearing them.

In the words of the children

If the wisdom of children were to truly be recognized, there would be more positive changes than we can imagine in all the world's cultures.

Children are very intuitive and aware of non-verbal communication and feelings. This sensitivity to others is a part of their wisdom. Children often express their wisdom in subtle ways that are missed by adults who are often in a more 'rational' world.

Six-year-old Salvina came to the demonstration group in Rome. When she went home, although she was quiet and said nothing of the workshop, she kept her warm fuzzy close to her and slept with it. The next day, she told her mother she would like to take her friend to the Kids' Workshop. Asked what she would tell her friend about the workshop, Salvina was thoughtful for a long time and then said: 'It is a place where children are understood and where they can be themselves.' Her statement expresses many things: trust of the environment and the facilitator, a feeling of security to be herself, and an ability to express her own wisdom. These come from the empathy of the facilitator and helper and their ability to put themselves in the child's place. Salvina, feeling that unconditional positive regard, recognized that she was free to express her wisdom and be creative.

Tim, age 10, attended DeSillio School in Colorado and said in a Kids' Workshop: 'I never knew about straight and mixed messages before. Now I understand myself and others better.'

Inviting other children to come to the Kids' Workshop in Rome, seven-year-old Maria wrote: 'In this day I am very calm and feel very good because an important thing happened. I found out how a double message makes me feel confused and a straight message makes me feel good. It is important for you to come so that you can feel good.'

Alicia, another seven-year-old in Rome, said: 'I would like for you to come, and I would like to show you how much power the workshop gives to you.'

An eight-year-old Navajo girl, Louise, said this after a fantasy exercise about a favorite place: 'My favorite place is high on a red rock where I can feel the wind blow and see the birds, like the eagle. I feel strong and free there. Now I know I will always have my favorite place wherever I go.' Her statement shows the security she feels knowing that her favorite place is a part of her and is always with her. Gypsy and refugee children also often express this feeling of security after the fantasy exercise. Although having an internal favorite place is important for all children, it is particularly important for children who move around. It gives them a sense of belonging.

Eight-year-old Roberto, from Rome, said: 'I have two favorite stories in the Kids' Workshop. One is the story of the

Warm Fuzzy and the other is the story of Spider Woman.[7] I ask you to come so that you may have much fun.'

A five-year-old girl from Saudi Arabia, Mina, said after a presentation: 'The Kids' Workshop was so much fun, and it made me feel good about myself.'

Laura, a 16-year-old girl in Italy, said: 'For me, the Kids' Workshop was truly beautiful. In the beginning maybe I was a little perplexed since I was the oldest one in the group. Then quickly I got comfortable. I felt good – in harmony with myself, with others, and aware of my emotions. I think that I will take with me all the time a "piece" of what this unusual day gave me.'

Antonio, a 10-year-old boy from Italy, said: 'One day I participated in a kids' group – a place in which finally adults understand children. I drew, I danced, and I felt good. I did have a lot of fun and did not want to go back home.'

Lucia, a teacher in Naples who presented the Kids' Workshop for Gypsy children living on the street and in a camp, said: 'The children became very involved in the Kids' Workshop activities, unlike other things we had presented to them, where they paid little attention. They wanted to

---

7. Spider Woman is a Navajo story about a woman who spins many threads of the rainbow that connects all of the world's living things – the animals, the birds, the trees and plants, and people of all colors and cultures from all four directions of the earth. All are one, and Mother Earth takes care of them all, as we take care of her. We are reminded every time we see a rainbow that we are all connected to one another. While Spider Woman's story is being told, the children stand in a circle and toss a skein of rainbow-colored yarn to one another. When a child catches it, she says how she feels at that moment and holds onto her piece of yarn while tossing the skein on to someone else. When it is completed, there is a beautiful rainbow web, and the children realize how we are all connected to each other. Children really enjoy this activity. They realize the beauty of diversity and the value of taking care of the earth and the environment.

repeat the Kids' Workshop over and over. Afterward they were much more calm and self-confident, and in school they were more interested and worked more on their studies.'

A 10-year-old girl from India, Sasha, said: 'I played with the puppets and I liked the Warm Fuzzies. I had many favorite animals that I drew – father, mother, and young swan, and the others were a peacock, a horse, a polar bear, and a dog. They all made me feel good about myself in different ways.'

This came from Elisa, age seven, in Rome: 'Kids' Workshop is a play because you get to have a lot of fun: you run, you play, make drawings, listen to stories, and create Warm Fuzzies. I keep my Warm Fuzzies from the workshop always with me, and when I see them they fill me with joy. I liked a lot playing with puppets because I got to play with the other children. Barbara Williams is a nice person who I was successful in understanding, even if she spoke English and I do not. I could understand her because she was calm and spoke slowly and it was nice that she was sitting on the floor with us. She was nice when she asked to be excused for not speaking Italian. The workbook I took home is fun because I can draw on it and show it to other children who do not know the Kids' Workshop. I learned how to talk to other people and that you do not need to fight and bicker.'

A five-year-old boy from Iran, Hakim, told us: 'I liked most the Warm Fuzzies. They made me feel good, and it is fun to give them to other people.'

Philippe, a nine-year-old boy from Paris, France, said: 'I liked being here. I had a lot of fun. I was very joyful.'

Also from Paris, 10-year-old Patrick was very active, and said: 'The methods of relaxation are really good.'

For Marta, an eight-year-old girl from Rome: 'The Kids' Workshop is a place where we children can be ourselves. We draw, we amuse ourselves, we listen, and we relax and look within ourselves.'

Sabrina, an eight-year-old girl from Florence, wrote in a note to me: 'Barbara, your idea is fantastic. I love the Kids' Workshop.'

Luciano, a nine-year-old boy from northern Italy, wrote: 'The Kids' Workshop has many activities very beautifully made in a place where friendship is not missing. The activity I liked best has been to make the drawing of the animal who made me feel well.'

Richard Donaldson, whose background is in philosophy and psychology, has observed the Kids' Workshop for 30 years. In his paper 'The Kids' Workshop: applications of the theories of Carl Rogers to working with children', he writes:

> *Training others to facilitate Kids' Workshops has increased*
> *awareness of the tremendous insights and benefits of*
> *person-centered ways of being. The use of these ideas*
> *in working with children has captured the attention of*
> *people around the world who are discovering that children*
> *are born with a profound way of being... that must be*
> *nurtured... Being taught what adults 'should be like' often*
> *destroys that way of being. The Kids' Workshop is an*
> *important way to nurture the profound child.*
> (Unpublished paper)

The children who have been involved in the Kids' Workshop will be able to think for themselves in life and know what they want and make their own decisions and have the confidence that they can carry them out and that will continue throughout their lifetime. They also will keep their creativity as they grow, and they will be close to nature, which will help them to be in touch with their own wisdom.

Part 5

Conclusion

In North America, children are among the groups most discriminated against. They are far down on politicians' lists of campaigning priorities. Politicians do not promote services for children that would provide protection and an environment where they can truly grow and change and prevent problems. People who work with children also experience discrimination: their salaries are often low and too often people assume they only work with children because they can't do anything else. Child abuse and child suicide is increasing. Too often, children are put in detention homes or even jails because there are no other programs for them, and their problems only become worse. Many children run away and live on the street because of problems with parents who don't know 'how to handle them'.

What if the adult world recognized the wisdom of children?

We would like to end here with our vision of what the world might be like if adults recognized the wisdom of children.

In education

Politicians would support programs to give teachers the skill to recognize children's wisdom and to establish schools where those teachers could give children support and space for learning in their own way. Each child would be recognized as an individual person and feel worthwhile. Suicide rates and dropout rates would decline.

Politicians would campaign for school administrators who were trained in these values and for contractors who could build schools with these values in mind. For example, school architecture has been much the same for decades. At one point, educators believed that there should be no windows in schools, so children could concentrate better. In his book *The Power of Design*, Richard Farson (2008) notes that architects can create bright, airy spaces with views of nature and that this environment leads to higher achievement and increased creativity in students.

The natural world is important to humans. Studies have shown that if children are taught in environments with access to or even just views of green spaces, there are huge benefits for their emotional, social, academic and psychological development (for an overview of some of this research, see Strife & Downey, 2009). If politicians wished to support children's development, they would support the building of schools that help to sustain children's growth. Architects could design schools with integrated gardens and open spaces and windows and doors that let children look outside.

> *Learning about the natural world should be treated as one of the most important events in children's lives.*
> (Louv, 2008)

> *Let Nature be your teacher.*
> (Wordsworth, 1888)

The learning environment would support teachers, and students, and all would enjoy the educational process and see its benefits. Children would be helped to concentrate and express their wisdom in their own way and would be less disruptive, more attentive, and less likely to 'need' drugs. How many millions of dollars would be saved on drugs if schools like this became mainstream?

Politicians would campaign for more counseling staff positions so children who needed it could have individual attention. Children would feel confident within themselves and would be less inclined to use alcohol or social drugs to boost their courage; they would enjoy life, spend time with friends, or go to school. How much money would be saved on new jails, prisons and other confinement centers? A high percentage of adolescents and young adults who end up in prison would instead have been tested early and found to be gifted or to have learning difficulties or attention deficit hyperactivity disorder (ADHD). In settings that recognize their individuality and unique learning styles, they would be on a path toward becoming happy and productive adults instead of 'social misfits' or criminals. Parents would be happy because their children would be happy and learning. And politicians would feel they were succeeding at an important and worthwhile job.

In DeSillio children were able to express their wisdom because of the support and freedom and respect for their wisdom shown by the teachers, other children, parents and the DeSillio community. The qualities of trust, empathy, acceptance and congruence that the children naturally had were respected and supported by the teachers, and the children were able to deepen these qualities and to express them. The teachers were very aware of the qualities in themselves and expressed them so they were positive models for the children. When we had problems in communication between teachers or teachers and parents or the community, it was usually because of lack of trust, congruence or acceptance.

We found that children who had been taking behavior-modification drugs in other schools were able to learn without drugs at DeSillio and grow emotionally, with confidence and high self-esteem. Much more exploration could be done in this area.

In DeSillio none of our children were on medication for psychological problems or behavior management. Each teacher was aware of each child and his or her background, learning styles, possible emotional problems and academic progress. The teachers met weekly to discuss each child and how he or she was doing. The school was designed so that, when a child was 'hyperactive', had trouble concentrating or had some 'behavior problem' or learning difficulty, a teacher was aware of it and could find resources that would help. These resources would be to help the child to be aware of themselves and what they needed and they could talk to any teacher at any time. As we stated before, Rough Rock is set up in much the same way, and less than five per cent of their children are on prescription drugs for any reason.

More evidence is coming out that many drugs can do damage, both physically and emotionally. The child loses confidence that they can learn or 'behave properly' without the use of drugs, and their self-esteem goes down and they feel that there is something wrong with them as a person. They feel that they have a label, such as ADHD, and once you have a label, it is like being put into a box, and it is hard to get out. Then, in teenage and adulthood, it is very easy to believe that a drug will solve any problem that they might have. In fact, they may feel that they need drugs to be able to live a life like anyone else, so one drug after another may be used, including alcohol and harmful social drugs. Creativity cannot but be damaged when you cannot express your hyperactivity and energy and the creative thought that is behind that.

Some of the most talented people that I know were very hyperactive when they were young. They were not told their hyperactivity was wrong, and that has helped them express energy and creativity as an adult. Ken Meinhart, a psychiatrist, was hyperactive as a child. He never let that interfere with his enthusiasm for life and his creativity. He went on to become a leading psychiatrist in the area and head of the mental health program in a large county in California. He was known for his innovative ideas and programs. Throughout his career as a psychiatrist, he was a fine woodworker and created beautiful objects, such as an organ and a harpsichord. He was also one of the most calm, accepting and empathetic people I have ever known. His hyperactivity as an adult took the form of having a lot of energy and creativity. He was grateful for that fact that he had been hyperactive as a child and as an adult, and people had respected that, and he was never put down, 'treated for it' or made to feel that it was wrong. He felt that it never interfered with his life but, on the contrary, greatly added to it.

Social services
If politicians campaigned for changes that recognize the wisdom of children, more money would be provided to state and county child welfare agencies so caseworkers would have smaller caseloads and more time to devote to each

child. With this kind of support, at-risk children would be much more likely to reach their highest potential and grow into responsible, independent adults who are not in danger of becoming part of the prison population. Directors of child welfare and other human services departments would be required to have a postgraduate degree in social work. With this preparation, they would understand the program and its needs and would have the skills to meet those needs. Competent social workers would be attracted to the field of human services; managers and directors would recognize these first rate qualities when hiring and would be able to offer high quality supervision and support.

As it stands now, nearly every county child welfare agency lacks the money to run a program that meets children's needs to feel secure, work on their problems in depth and reach their highest potential. Too often children end up in jails and prisons because they drop out of school, get involved with drugs and alcohol, and have low-paying jobs (or cannot get jobs) and low self-confidence. Because of lack of money, caseworkers have extremely high caseloads; they cannot meet with each child, evaluate each situation, and give the child the time and support he or she needs to grow. Too often, time, money and energy are spent trying to put a Band-Aid on the problem or find a fast solution, rather than working toward a long-term solution of real value to the child.

Highly qualified social workers generally do not go into human services because of low pay and because they feel they cannot really help children in the system as it stands today. In the US, most social workers with graduate degrees go into private practice as psychotherapists because that is where their skills are most appreciated. Many caseworkers lack a social work degree and are not qualified to work with children who have serious problems or who live in challenging situations. These caseworkers miss many problems, including child abuse.

At this time, many directors of departments do not have a degree in social work. Their background is often in business administration. They do not have the knowledge to evaluate the social problems children have and to work out solutions. Therefore, it is difficult for them to recognize those qualities in the staff they hire and to support their staff. Sometimes they are threatened by highly qualified social workers. I worked as a social worker in child welfare the summer before I received my degree, and received high ratings from my supervisor. The summer after I received my degree, I applied for a caseworker position in the child welfare department of my county, knowing demand was high and many positions were open. I applied for a position and, to my dismay, was turned down. A friend who happened to be at the hiring committee meeting later told me that one of the county commissioners had said, 'Don't hire social workers with degrees; they're troublemakers.'

Foster homes
There is a great need for good foster homes that can help and support children after they have had traumatic experiences. If politicians and people in general realized the great need for good homes for children and the almost unbelievable ways that a good, insightful, positive, accepting foster home can help a child and change a child's life, foster homes would be recognized as of great importance. Money would be provided for highly qualified social workers to look for good, supportive homes, and they would interview

foster parents very carefully to understand their needs and why they wanted to be a foster parent. To be a good foster parent requires extremely hard work and dedication, and you have to be emotionally stable to withstand the tests that the children put you through 'to see if you really love me and believe in me and will not reject me like everyone else in my life has'. This is the message that most foster children have and it is very seldom verbalized. I have heard many times from foster children that I have worked with in psychotherapy, 'I must be a bad person or people would not distrust me so much and treat me so badly and reject me. I think that I was born bad.' I have heard three-year-old children say this, as well as 16-year-olds.

Money would be provided for extensive training programs and continued support groups for foster parents. This would be a strong prevention program that would help foster parents stay in the program and not reject child after child, and it would help them to work with the schools and people in the community to support their child. After the training was complete, the social worker would carefully match each foster child with a foster parent so that their needs would meet and it could be a positive placement, lasting as long as the child needed the support. Officials would recognize that these children had suffered much rejection and traumatic experiences and that, for the child to overcome these emotional shocks, they need strong, long-lasting support to feel loved, accepted and self-confident and to be able to grow into independent, responsible adults and reach their highest potential. Under these circumstances, foster children could have a positive experience and their lives would be changed. Millions of dollars would be saved by these children not being in jails and detention centers.

Parents

Most people want to be good parents, and they can be if they have the tools and resources. More resources would be provided, such as parenting workshops, workshops before the arrival of a child and ongoing workshops where parents can become more aware of children's wisdom and the person-centered approach. Parents would understand their importance in children's lives. There would be less child abuse, fewer runaways living on the streets, and fewer children in institutions.

In a warm and supportive environment the child, beginning in infancy, can bring his or her innate wisdom to consciousness and express it. Parents and other adults may not welcome a child's wisdom or feel comfortable receiving it. Nevertheless, they must be strong in their resolve to trust the children – to help them to know and express their wisdom and to protect them when others do not understand.

A parent has the greatest opportunity to provide a secure environment in which their child can come to recognize his or her own wisdom. A parent can be the child's companion in exploring the larger world, and their refuge if they meet someone there who does not recognize their gifts or – even unintentionally – tries to destroy them.

People in general would recognize children's wisdom and present laws to protect it and encourage it in every area. People would be aware of different cultures and different countries and the need to help the children of those different countries recognize and protect their wisdom, and they would be aware of the richness these children of the world could give to the world if they were encouraged in their wisdom and protected. Children would be empowered in every way. Politicians would realize the value, beauty and richness of differences and different ways of expressing things, and they would not be afraid of them. People would be more aware of the damage war does to all children, even those not directly involved in it, and there would be a greater chance for peace in the world.

> *We see a new world around us. We have the impression that we are at the dawn of a new period... those who are young in mind and spirit – and that often means those who are young in body as well.*
>
> *Where will they come from?*
>
> *It is my observation that they already exist.*
> (Rogers, 1980)

The Kids' Workshop can bring all of these things together and can truly help children to express their wisdom.

What is a Kids' Workshop? In the words of the children, it is: 'A place where we children can be ourselves. We draw, we amuse ourselves, we listen, and we relax and look within ourselves;' 'A place in which finally adults understand children;' 'A place where children are understood and where they can be themselves.'

If children's wisdom were truly recognized, there would be amazing changes in cultures all over the world.

'Listen to us – just listen to us and respect our ideas.'

The Navajo word for goodbye in translation is, 'May you walk in beauty.' That means, may you be in harmony with yourself, with other people, with nature, with all cultures of the world and with the universe. This is a poem from the Navajo ceremony, the Beauty Way.

May you walk in beauty

I am a child of the Earth
I am a child of the Sky
I am a child of the Universe
There is Beauty above me
There is Beauty below me
There is Beauty within me
There is Beauty all around me
May I walk in Beauty

May all of the children of the universe walk in Beauty.

Bibliography

Andreas S (1991). *Virginia Satir: the pattern of her magic.* Palo Alto, CA: Science and Behavior Books Inc.

Andreas S (2002). *Transforming Your Self: becoming who you want to be.* Boulder, CO: Real People Press.

Axline VM (1964). *Dibs in Search of Self.* New York: Ballatine Books, Inc.

Axline VM (1947, Italian edition 2009, with an introduction by Alberto Zucconi). *Play Therapy.* Rome: La Meridiana.

Bahti T, Bahti M (1997). *Southwestern Indian Ceremonials.* Wickenburg, AZ: KC Publications, Inc.

Behr M, Cornelius-White JHD (2008). *Facilitating Young People's Development: International Perspectives on Person-Centered Theory and Practice.* Ross-on-Wye: PCCS Books.

Bratton S, Ray D, Edwards N, Landreth G (2010). Child-Centered Play Therapy (CCPT): theory, research, and practice. *Journal of Person-Centered and Experiential Psychotherapies 8*(4): 266–281.

Caduto M, Bruchac J (1989). *Keepers of the Earth.* Golden, CO: Fulcrum Inc.

Caduto M, Bruchac J (1991). *Keepers of the Animals: Native American stories and wildlife activities for children.* Golden, CO: Fulcrum Inc.

Cornelius-White JHD, Motschnig-Pitrik R, Lux M (eds) (2013). *Interdisciplinary Applications of the Person-Centered Approach.* New York: Springer.

De Peretti F (2013). Kids' Workshop. *Le Trait d'Union 26.*

Donaldson R (undated). *The Kids' Workshop: applications of the theories of Carl Rogers to working with children.* (Unpublished paper, available from the author at page@quesnelbc.com).

Dreikus R (1964). *Children: the challenge.* New York, NY: Hawthorn Books Inc.

Farson RE (1974). *Birth Rights: a bill of rights for children.* New York: Macmillan.

Farson RE (2008). *The Power of Design: a force for transforming everything.* Norcross, GA: Greenway Communications.

Farson (R) 2010. *Will All Parenting Experts Please Leave the Room! Paradoxes in parenting.* La Jolla, CA: Western Behavioral Sciences Institute.

Farson R, with Keyes R (2002). *Whoever Makes the Most Mistakes Wins: the paradox of innovation.* New York: The Free Press.

Hooker K (2002). *Time among the Navajo.* Flagstaff, AZ: Salina Bookshelf Inc.

Johnson BH (1968). *Navajo Education at Rough Rock.* (Rough Rock, AZ: Rough Rock Demonstration School.

Kirschenbaum H (1979). *On Becoming Carl Rogers.* New York City, NY: Delacorte Press.

Louv R (2008). *Last Child in the Woods: saving our children from nature-deficient disorder* (revised and updated edition). Chapel Hill, North Carolina: Algonquin Books.

McKee P, Barber C (1999). On defining wisdom. *The International Journal of Aging and Human Development 49*(2): 149–164.

Oaklander V (1978). *Windows to Our Children: a Gestalt therapy approach to children and adolescents.* Moab, UT: Real People Press.

Page J, Page S (1982). *Navajo.* New York: Abrams.

Rogers CR (1951). *Client-Centered Therapy.* Boston: Houghton Mifflin.

Rogers CR (1961). *On Becoming a Person: a therapist's view of psychotherapy.* Boston: Houghton Mifflin.

Rogers CR (1969). *Freedom to Learn: a view of what education might become.* Columbus, Ohio: Charles E. Merrill Publishing Co.

Rogers CR (1980). *A Way of Being.* Boston: Houghton Mifflin.

Rogers CR (1983). *Freedom to Learn for the 80's.* Columbus, Ohio: Charles E. Merrill Publishing Co.

Rogers CR, Stevens B (1967). *Person to Person: the problem of being human.* Lafayette, CA: Real People Press.

Rogers N (1993). *The Creative Connection: expressive arts as healing.* Palo Alto, CA. Science & Behavior Books Inc.

Satir V (1975). *Self-Esteem.* Millbrae, CA: Celestial Arts.

Satir V (1976). *Making Contact.* Millbrae, CA: Celestial Arts.

Satir V (1988). *The New Peoplemaking* (2nd edition). Palo Alto, CA: Science and Behavior Books.

Satir V (2000). *In Famiglia... come va? Vivere le relazioni in modo significativo.* Aqui Terme Al: Impressioni Grafiche.

Simonelli JM, Winters CD (1997). *Crossing Between Worlds: the Navajo of Canyon de Chelly.* Santa Fe, NM: School of American Research Press.

Steiner C (1977). *The Original Warm Fuzzy Tale*. Sacramento, CA: Jalmar Press.

Stevens B (1970). *Don't Push the River*. Moab, UT: The Real People Press.

Strife S, Downey L (2009). Childhood development and access to nature: a new direction for environmental inequality research. *Organization & Environment 22*(1): 99–122.

Williams B (1992). Kids: a profound way of being. Presentation at the Person-Centred Forum, La Jolla, California, August 1987. *Da Persona a Person – Rivista di Studi Rogersiani*. www.acp-italia.it/rivista/1992/ Barbara_williams_-_kids_a_profound_way_of_being.pdf (accessed 17 June 2016).

Wordsworth W (1888). 'The Tables Turned'. In: Wordsworth W. *The Complete Poetical Works*. London: Macmillan & Co.

Zucconi A (2007). *From Illness to Health, Well-being and Empowerment: the person-centered paradigm shift from patient to client*. Rome: Istituto dell'Approccio Centrato sulla Persona (IACP).

Zucconi A, Howell P (2001). *Health Promotion: using the person-centered approach to integrate the bio-psycho-social model*. Rome: Istituto dell'Approccio Centrato sulla Persona (IACP).

Websites

www.kids-workshop.com

Kid's Workshop International has its own Facebook page. Search for Kids' Workshop International Facebook.

www.pcafrance.com

www.roughrock.bia.edu

www.social.iacp.it

Index

CPSIA information can be obtained at www.ICGtesting.com
Printed in the USA
LVOW10s2138160916

504806LV00002B/2/P

9 781910 919200